# "G-O-O-D-Y"

A Memoir on Service from Greenwood to Redan and Throughout the Baseball Community

Gregory "Goody" Goodwin

With

Harold Michael Harvey

Front Cover design by Harold Michael Harvey
Front Cover Photograph The Goodwin Collection
Back Cover Photograph The Goodwin Collection
Back Cover Design Harold Michael Harvey

Cascade Publishing House
1315 Desoto Falls Court, SW
Atlanta, Georgia 30311

We are in the business of writing and publishing

Copyright © 2022 by Gregory Goodwin

All rights are reserved, including the right to reproduce this book or portions thereof in any form For information, contact the publisher above.

ISBN: 978-0-9975346-7-2

Library of Congress Control Number: 2022912929

*Myke,*
*Continued blessings*
*Peace + Love*
*Greg Dad*
*11-3-22*

Manufactured in the United States of America

# Dedication

This book I dedicate to my mother, Alquita Joy Goodwin, and my father, Edward Lawrence Goodwin, Jr., my lottery ticket to a beautiful life.

Our parents would be pleased with how their kids are giving back to their individual communities.

Sabrina followed her brother's decision to attend Tennessee State University where she served as Ms. TSU in 1982. Currently, Sabrina enjoys her career as a National Sales Director with Mary Kay Cosmetics.

She is married to Kenny Monday, 1996 Olympic Gold Medalist in Wrestling, and they are the parents of Sydnee, Kennedy, and Quincy.

The youngest sister, Regina is a University of Kansas graduate. She recently completed her 7th year serving District 73 (the district where we grew up) in the Oklahoma House of Representatives.

Our brother Eric, before his untimely death, served Coretta Scott King as Coordinator at the King Center for Non-Violent Social Change.

# Table of Content

DEDICATION .................................................................. III
REFLECTIONS ON "GOODY" ................................................ V
FOREWORD.................................................................. VIII
PART ONE
LEGACY ............................................................................ 2
PART TWO
GREENWOOD ................................................................. 49
PART THREE
LAND OF THE GOLDEN SUNSHINE................................. 106
PART FOUR
GATE CITY ..................................................................... 140
PART FIVE
DREAM MAKER.............................................................. 170
POSTSCRIPT ...................................................................210
PHOTOGRAPHS..............................................................212
ABOUT THE AUTHOR .....................................................226
ABOUT THE EDITOR ......................................................227

# REFLECTIONS ON "GOODY"

In a word, Greg Goodwin is:

**"Big-hearted."**

Roger Cador, former head baseball coach, Southern University and Inductee to the American Baseball Coaches Association and Louisiana Sports Hall of Fame

**"Difference-maker."**

Sam Hughes, National Cross-Checker New York Yankees

**"Resourceful."**

Marque Denmon, Professional Live Sports, and Entertainment Announcer

**"Passion."**

Steve Williams, Senior Director of Player Development, Pittsburg Pirates and President, Buck O'Neil Professional Scouts, and Coaches Association

**"Accommodating"**

Bernard Pattillo, former Director of Recreation, City of Atlanta

**"Pioneering."**

Marquis Grissom, former professional baseball player

**"Fun."**

Sabrina Goodwin Monday, National Sales Director, Mary Kay Cosmetics [Sister]

**"Fearless."**

Robert Goodwin, Former CEO, Points of Light, former Director of the Whitehouse Initiative for HBCUs, U. S. Department of Education (Uncle)

"G-O-O-D-Y"

**"Benevolent"**

Regina Goodwin, State Representative, District 73, Oklahoma [Sister]

# Foreword

A Poem

By Kriste Young, former PTA President, Redan High School

To know him is to love him; to know his heart is to know God.
    To hear of him is to be grateful
To meet him is to be encouraged
To know Him is to know God's heart and be inspired.

Greg humbly serves, never seeking recognition or accolades. Greg Goodwin is a living example and defines "Ordinary People, Doing Extraordinary Things," the motto he served under while Principal at RHS. His heart and hands of service always reach beyond the individual and impact families to shift the narrative for generations to come.

To read about him is to seek your better self
And challenge yourself to give in a way that
rises breathing. In the words of Greg:
"It's not rocket science, do it for the kids!"

"It's about the kids."

Gregory "Goody" Goodwin

# Part One
# Legacy

"G-O-O-D-Y"

*"If my great grandparents Carlie and J. H. Goodwin, as well as my grandfather E. L. Goodwin, Sr., had not survived the Tulsa Race Massacre of 1921, I would not be here today to render my service to humankind."*

Gregory "Goody" Goodwin

My name is "Goody." I was born Gregory Parker Goodwin in Independence, Kansas, in 1957 because there was no hospital in Cherryvale, Kansas, where my mom lived. Cherryvale is about twenty miles from the Oklahoma border, my dad's home state. Fewer than 3,000 people lived in Cherryvale, Kansas, the year I was born. The population of Cherryvale is now 2,192. Hard to believe I had more students in the high school [Redan] I worked for in Stone Mountain, Georgia, for 30-plus years than in the city of my birth.

According to the 1960 census, Cherryvale had 2,783 people, down from 2,952 recorded in the 1950 census. Less than one percent of the population is African American. The town, from the start, has had more Native Americans than Black Americans. The most famous person in Cherryvale the year I was born was Vivian Vance, the actress who played Ethel Mertz on the *I Love Lucy* sitcom.

Because my mom lived in Cherryvale, I was born a "Jayhawker" and not a "Sooner." I'm not sure what to make of this quirk of geopolitical genealogy.

Without a doubt, I am an Oklahoman in the true spirit of the frontier. My daddy, Edward Lawrence Goodwin, Jr., was known professionally as E. L. Goodwin. His parents, Edward Lawrence Goodwin, Sr. and Jeanne Osby Goodwin, raised him to give back to his community.

In the second generation of freedom after the Civil War, many Black men, like my great grandfather, J. H. Goodwin, and my grandfather, E. L. Goodwin, Sr., used their initials in professional settings to prevent white people from referring to them by their first name.

White people had a habit of calling Black people by their first name. Whites seldom, if ever, used the term Mr. or Mrs. when getting the attention of a Black person.

Black people, the men particularly, detested this act of racial insensitivity. To get around this dehumanizing tactic, many Blacks would sign legal documents with their initials so that Whites would not know their names and therefore could not disrespect them by calling them by their first name.

Given the times he grew up, it came as no surprise that my father would sign his name as E. L. Goodwin, Jr. as he grew into manhood. My daddy had several nicknames, including Lil Ed, Gooney, Gump, 802, and Junior.

He was a good-natured man who sought to help people every chance he got. One of the nicknames that stuck to him was "Goody."

Not only was this nickname a play on the family name Goodwin, but Daddy always found a way to do something good for the people he met. He constantly and consistently helped other people in the dilemmas confronting them. He never met a stranger, so it did not take him long to figure out if he was going to "extend the right hand of fellowship" to someone he had just met. In good times and in bad times, my daddy found creative ways to serve other people.

My family did not call me "Goody" after my dad. In our family, that name belonged to my father. My father's peers referred to him as "Goody," and often referred to my brother Eric and I as "Little Goody."

Several members of the Goodwin clan have been called "Goody" by their friends at one time or another. I have cousins, nieces, and nephews called "Goody" by their friends and professional associates.

I came about the moniker "Goody" quite by accident. Family and friends called me Greg, or "Lil Greg" – yes, I was small in stature as a kid - until I reached college and was a baseball team member.

I grew five inches and gained forty pounds between my high school graduation and my freshman year of college. My teammates started calling me "Goody" in middle school. I played baseball, football, and basketball in middle school. I am unsure if my teammates heard their fathers call my dad **"Goody."**

Maybe they did.

My daddy was athletic when I was growing up. He enjoyed playing basketball and being a lefty; he was a baseball pitcher during his youth. It was natural that the guys on the playground would think of me as "Goody," too.

The nickname stuck, and I have tried since then to live up to the reputation of "Goody," Sr. I make no monopolistic claim to the nickname "Goody" among members of the Goodwin family; nevertheless, in my circle of friends, I sometimes introduce myself as "Goody."

Perhaps I cannot make an exclusive claim to the name Goody because family folklore says that J. H. Goodwin changed his birth name Goldwyn to Goodwin when he became an adult.

The Goldwyn plantation in Water Valley, Mississippi, was home to my great grandmother Sallie Williams, a slave. We believed that the father of J. H. Goodwin was a slaveholder on the Goldwyn plantation in Water Valley, Mississippi. Whether I am good or gold, it's all good.

In addition to honoring the family name, it reminds me that my purpose in life is to do good like my daddy and win doing good, as Goodwin implies. I play the good game of life to win over friends and influence others to do good in the world.

My mother, Alquita, was in high school when my parents met. An introduction came from her older brother, Harold Parker, my daddy's fraternity brother.

They sang in the choir known as the Choraleers during their college years. Mama and her siblings attended an integrated school system in Cherryvale, Kansas. Bethel and Harold Parker, Sr.'s home was located at 229 E. 7th Street. I spent my first three years there and received a ton of love before moving to Tulsa in 1960.

I would surmise my athletic talent came from family genes donated from the Parkers. All my mom's brothers were high school star athletes and played basketball collegiately.

Uncle Harold was the first Black basketball player at Independence Community College in Independence, Kansas. Uncle Davey played at Texas Southern University, and Uncle Jerry played at Coffeyville Community College.

## "G-O-O-D-Y"

Mama's sisters, Aunt Wanda and Aunt Charlotte were phenomenal women and my mama, the baby of the Parker women, followed in her sisters' footsteps. I was blessed to have been nurtured by them.

Mama was the disciplinarian in our family. She kept my older brother, Eric, my younger sisters, Sabrina, Regina, and myself in line. We were allowed to have a lot of fun but being disrespectful and not respecting our elders was not tolerated. Mama remains the best advice giver and cook I have ever known. Mama did not have to take the belt to us much; after a "cool" look or nod of the head, we understood to straighten up. We had a great childhood. In 1957, the year I was born, my father graduated from Pittsburg State University in Pittsburg, Kansas, with a degree in journalism. He was twenty-two years old. All he had ever known was the newspaper business.

While in school at Pittsburg State, he traveled back home to Tulsa at least three days a week to help his father run the family-owned newspaper. You could say that newspapering was in his blood.

He became fascinated with the newspaper business because his grandfather J. H. (James Henri) Goodwin and his father were in the newspaper business.

In 1916, my great-grandfather, J. H. Goodwin went to work as the finance manager for *The Tulsa Star,* owned by a prominent Black newspaperman named A. J. (Andrew Jackson) Smitherman.

*The Tulsa Star* originated in Muskogee, Oklahoma, in 1912 when Smitherman decided to leave his employ with the *Muskogee Cimeter.* He served four years as the paper's traveling agent and advertising manager. He sought to lend his voice to a different editorial direction than the Muskogee Cimeter's pro-Republican slant.

Smitherman was a Democrat in an era when Black Americans, forty-seven years removed from enslavement, strongly favored Republican public policy initiatives.

Please, do not make a mistake about it; Smitherman was pro-Black America. His masthead proclaimed: "A Fearless Exponent of Right and Justice," "An Uncompromising Defender of the Colored Race," and "We Fear Only To Do Wrong."

My great-grandfather, J. H. Goodwin, and Smitherman respected one another from the start. When my great-grandfather boarded a train in the early 1910s in Water Valley, Mississippi, they met by chance heading for Iowa.

My great-grandfather left Mississippi and a successful funeral home business and a general store in downtown Water Valley, a small town of around 4,000 people, according to the 1940 census. He searched for a school district for his children that went further than the fifth-grade education he received in Mississippi. He thought Iowa was that place.

As the train meandered from Mississippi into St. Louis, my great-grandfather noticed a man holding a sign at a train depot extolling the virtue of living in Tulsa, Oklahoma. On the spot, he decided to visit Tulsa first. In Tulsa, he met Smitherman, who inquired about my great grandfather's travels.

When Smitherman learned of J. H. Goodwin's desire to raise his family in a wholesome environment, he told him about the affluent Greenwood area in North Tulsa. A growing community of about 11,000 Black people, in a city of around 18,000. He quickly did the math.

A town of 11,000 people potentially would need the services of a mortician more frequently than a town of 4,000. My great-grandfather knew how to make money, but more importantly, he knew how to manage his finances. It did not take Smitherman long to bring my grandfather into the newspaper business as his business manager.

He maintained the books using sound accounting principles he learned through common sense and a command of arithmetic.

He opened several businesses in the Greenwood district, including a funeral home, a variety store, an office building, and several rooming houses.

His financial assets increased, and his stature in the community rose to influential heights.

In 1917, J. H. Goodwin was a founding director of the Booker T. Washington Hospital.

The hospital was incorporated on May 7, 1917: "to conduct a general hospital for the sick and afflicted; to render prompt and efficient aid to those who, through accident or misfortune, are seriously injured; to provide adequate and proper instruction to those who would qualify themselves for trained nurses; and to provide for suffering humanity through proper medical aid."

He served as vice president of the Booker T. Washington Hospital. He served alongside Tulsa's leading citizens like Charles H. Tucker, P. S. Thompson, J. H. Key, William Walker, A. E. S. Wright, Mathew Frazier, Mrs. H. H. Robinson, and Mrs. Caroline Lollio.

According to the 1920 census, the population of Tulsa had swelled from 18,182 to 72,075. Mainly on the strength of the oil reserves found in Tulsa at the turn of the century.

From 1916 to 1921, under the business management of my great grandfather, *The Tulsa Star* thrived. On January 15, 1921, Smitherman announced that the newspaper had relocated to 126 ½ Greenwood Avenue on the corner of Greenwood Avenue and Brady Street.

Smitherman began 1921 with great expectations for the future growth of his publishing empire.

According to the announcement, the newspaper's new home was "the largest and most complete newspaper and printing establishment in the country for members of our group except for the Baptist Publishing House in Nashville."

Two months after moving into its new office and two months before Memorial Day 1921, Smitherman brought Dr. W. E. B. DuBois to Tulsa. Little did DuBois know that in two months, his words would prove to be prophetic.

According to Steve Gerkin in a piece titled *First Charged, Last Freed*, Dubois told the Greenwood community: "When the armed lynchers come, we too must gather armed. When the mob moves, we propose to meet it with sticks and clubs and guns."

DuBois was on a tour of the country, ramping up support for his anti-lynching campaign. While the white press did not cover his speech in Tulsa, words spoken by the great orator spread like wildfire. Black soldiers who had fought in World War I strutted around town in their military uniforms bearing arms at the sound of lynch mob talk.

One hundred and thirty-five days after moving to the corner of Greenwood Avenue and Brady Street, *The Tulsa Star* goes up in flames.

It went up in flames along with all the Black-owned businesses and homes on Greenwood Avenue and in North Tulsa when a white South Tulsa mob moved across the railroad tracks onto Greenwood Avenue.

Ostensibly, they claimed to avenge a 17-year-old white girl who the gang believed to have suffered a sexual attack from a 19-year-old Black man. This alleged incident sparked what would become the 1921 Tulsa Race Massacre. The bloody tragic event was initially deemed a race riot so that the numerous insurance claims did not have to be honored.

The girl never came forth to swear out an arrest warrant, and she refused to attend a grand jury hearing to testify against her alleged assailant. The unspoken truth among Black Tulsans was that a Black man tripped getting onto the elevator and was hurled into the white girl tearing her dress as he attempted to keep his balance.

Other people talked about a romantic relationship in which the two were involved, regardless the names Dick Rowland and Sara Page would forever be linked to the elevator incident that occurred in the Drexel Building in May of 1921.

The girl yelled.

Then she emerged from the elevator she operated in the office building; the hem of her dress was torn. The whites concluded that the Black man on the elevator had molested her.

All hell broke loose. Years of envy of Black prosperity in North Tulsa boiled over. "It was time to put those wealthy, uppity Negroes of North Tulsa in their place," seemed to be the guiding thought in the collective mind of Whites in South Tulsa.

Given the enthusiasm of the DuBois speech, Smitherman's home and publishing company burned in the blaze. Smitherman left Oklahoma and moved to Buffalo, New York.

All he had built, all he fought to achieve for Black people 50 years after enslavement, went up in flames with the entire North Tulsa community. He never returned to Oklahoma.

When the race massacre began, my great grandfather J. H. Goodwin, a very fair-complexioned man, grabbed his shotgun, slung it over one of his shoulders, and stood out in front of his home perched atop a hill.

He was determined to find a way to protect his property and family. As a maddening crowd of white men, their minatory countenance visible ten paces ahead of their steps, descended on him, he calmly pointed in the opposite direction of their locomotion and yelled:

*"Them Niggers went that way."*

The mob followed in the direction of what appeared to be a pointed White finger, and when the smoke cleared, the only house standing on the street was the home of J. H. Goodwin.

If my great-grandfather and his progeny had not survived the Tulsa Massacre of 1921, I would not be here today, and all the service I have rendered and that I will cause in the future would never have seen the light of day. I would not have been able to assist the thousands of young students in obtaining their high school diplomas. There would be no Goodwin name on the street in front of Redan High School.

Correspondingly, I couldn't continue the service to humankind begun by J. H. Goodwin of Water Valley, Mississippi, in Tulsa, Oklahoma.

Some people believe that Tuskegee Institute Principal Booker T. Washington dubbed Greenwood as the "The Negro Wall Street" following a visit to North Tulsa in 1905.

There is no conclusive record that Washington coined the phrase. We know that Washington visited North Tulsa and was impressed with the business community emerging independent of the business and trade conducted in the white section of Tulsa.

During his visit, Washington told business leaders about a community he developed in 1901 on the outskirts of the campus at Tuskegee Institute on a 4,000-acre tract of land in Alabama.

Washington created the Greenwood Community to encourage Blacks to become self-sufficient by owning and operating a farm. Washington hired his college classmate and roommate from Hampton Institute, Charles Wallace Green, to lay out the development. He named the community Greenwood in honor of Charles Wallace Green.

At the urging of O. W. Gurley, a wealthy Black man from Arkansas whose rooming house gave comfort to Blacks fleeing Jim Crow in Mississippi, and other southern states, Black Tulsans named their bustling economic street, Greenwood Avenue, or so it's been told.

Some historians believe that Greenwood Avenue received this name from Greenwood, Mississippi, to honor the many people from Mississippi who settled in the northern section of Tulsa. Gurley considered Oklahoma a significant economic and social opportunity.

This prevailing thought led to the establishment of many all-Black towns and settlements.

There were more Black towns and settlements organized in Oklahoma than in any state or territory in the country. The more than twenty All-Black towns in the mid-nineteenth through the turn of the twentieth century were bustling towns of "Black Pride."

Although many of these towns no longer exist, their legacy remains integral to the African American struggle for freedom, independence, and prosperity.

This settlement of the territory's All-Black towns can be tied to the Trail of Tears, the forced removal of Native Americans (1830-1850) from the country's southeastern region to Indian territory in the West.

Several African Americans who were held as slaves by the tribes made the journey to Indian Territory, as well. Of course, when Black Gold, i. e., oil was found on Indian Territory this land was quickly reclaimed by the United States government.

I'm not sure if this information would be considered "Critical Race Theory," but I do know it's the truth.

At the beginning of statehood in 1907, Oklahoma passed several laws. Among the first laws passed in the new state of Oklahoma (1907), thirty-three days after statehood was a Jim Crow system of legally forced segregation. The law required Blacks and Whites to live in separate areas.

Whether it was Gurley or Washington who named Greenwood Avenue, "The Negro (Black) Wall Street," the name stuck. More people came to witness what Black people could do if they were banned together in solidarity around circulating their money in their community.

Today that area between Greenwood, Archer, and Pine is proudly referred to as "The Black Wall Street." However, the site is only two blocks now.

When I was fondly living at 1415 North Greenwood as a child and growing up around Archer and Pine Streets, the locals referred to the area as North Tulsa. There was the Deep Greenwood section, the southern part of the street, and Shallow Greenwood located on the northern end of the street. I explored all of Greenwood as a youth. There was always more action – some good, some not good - on the deep end.

Unfortunately, that area has changed tremendously from when I was a youth. The Black Wall Street area has been reduced to only a couple of blocks, and its demise can be attributed to Urban Renewal, i. e., urban removal. This same fate seems to turn most urban Black communities across the country into ghost towns, or areas recreated by regentrification.

At the turn of the last century, Washington understood the importance of Greenwood. In addition to the Greenwood community in Tuskegee, he also attempted, with little success, to launch a farming community at what today is known as Hilton Head, South Carolina.

The two communities point out the difference between social welfare and a capitalist pursuit.

Washington provided the land, seeds, and farming instruments to freemen a few decades removed from enslavement in this Tuskegee experiment.

While the Greenwood community in Tuskegee is still a thriving community, the Hilton Head venture did not meet similar success. Washington found the people did not respect the property boundaries of their neighbors, taking their farm crops and animals and failing to keep an accurate account of the assets entrusted to them.

On Greenwood Avenue in Tulsa, a person earned what they acquired. Each person was responsible for obtaining and maintaining their level of wealth. Greenwood was a self-sufficient community where the residents took pride in living their best American dream.

After three days of white terror and rage over the Memorial Day weekend in 1921, "Black [Negro] Wall Street" was no more.

This once-thriving district of Black-owned businesses lay smoldering in ruins. The American dreams of so many, gone, not with the wind, but in a great plume of smoke; hopes dashed, lives lost, and the source of

Black pride on the great frontier buried in the ashes of Greenwood and North Tulsa.

Theodore Baughman, who served as managing editor of *The Tulsa Star* before forming his newspaper on June 20, 1927, secured Smitherman's printing press. After the white mob settled down, they reopened *The Tulsa Star* under the name of the *Oklahoma Eagle*.

My great-grandfather did not leave Tulsa after the race massacre. He stayed and immediately began the arduous task of rebuilding the social safety net of North Tulsa. Six months after the last ember flickered out, my great grandfather and ten other men invested $6,000 into establishing the Tulsa Colored Hospital Association of Tulsa, Oklahoma.

The black business incorporated the new hospital on December 22, 1921.

My great-grandfather's group filed the incorporation papers in the courthouse on January 3, 1922. The stated purpose of this hospital was to: "provide and keep a building for the housing, feeding, and treating sick persons… and maintained not for profit."

Black Tulsans named the new hospital after a white man, Marvin Willows, President of the Tulsa Red Cross.

The first Black hospital was named Booker T. Washington Hospital (1917-1921). It was built two years after the death of Washington, then destroyed in the fires of the Tulsa Race Massacre.

Staying in Tulsa after the 1921 Race Massacre, J. H. Goodwin lent stability to the rebuilding efforts undertaken by other men who did not run away from the Black Mecca they had built in the early days of the 20th century.

No one could blame survivors for leaving the area. The various insurance companies denied insurance claims because the courts deemed the Race Massacre a riot.

How ludicrous!

But the laws were made for and by racist White men during that time in our nation's history. There was no recourse for survivors.

One hundred years later, survivors and descendants of this tragic event still seek restitution in the courts.

Because J. H. Goodwin's home was largely untouched, he had a platform to aid in the rebuilding of the Greenwood business district.

His home became a haven for George Washington Carver, who continued the connection between Tuskegee Institute and Greenwood following the passing of Booker T. Washington in 1915.

On his visits to North Tulsa to speak and present an exhibit of the products he had invented from peanuts at the Negro Fair Association and schools in Greenwood, Carver stayed in J. H. and Carlie Goodwin's home owned by my great-grandparents.

Carver's first visit was in 1927, my great grandparents were in their fifties, and according to Peter Duncan Burchard, who writes in his book, *Carver: A Great Soul*, Carver's catalog contained: "two hundred and two" products made from the peanut, including "soap, shaving lotion, wood stains, dyes for cloth, milk, candles, coffee, powder for the face, and wallboard."

He describes my great grandmother Carlie Goodwin as "motherly, rounded and dark-complected."

She contrasted greatly with my great-grandfather J. H., who was a highly fair-complexioned man. He could have lived as an Irishman because of the blood that flowed in his veins, but he chose to live and work among Negro people whose blood he also carried.

Legally he had no choice because of the one-drop rule, a social and legal principle of racial classification that was prominent in the 20th century in the United States. It asserted that any person with even one blood drop of Black ancestry is considered Black, Negro, or Colored in historical terms.

Perhaps, my destiny included a career in education because, in 1927, the all-white Tulsa School Board superintendent learned that George Washington Carver was coming to Tulsa for the Negro Fair Association exhibit.

He sent a communique to my great-grandfather and asked him if he could arrange to have Carver come and speak privately with the White school board.

The principals of Booker T. Washington High School and Paul Laurence Dunbar Elementary School escorted Carver into a meeting with the superintendent and the Tulsa County School Board.

There had never been a meeting of this kind in the history of public education in Tulsa. No, not where Black educators met with elected school board members in Tulsa, not until October 7, 1927, when Carver mesmerized the White school board and what Burchard describes as "some of Tulsa's high-placed civic leaders."

Harry Abbott, Carver's secretary, would later characterize the meeting like this:

"For more than an hour, the gathering listened unusually attentively to the address of Dr. Carver, at the close of which he privileged them to ask questions. The group did and were marvelously enlightened."

At the week's end, Carver spoke to Black Tulsans in an insurance building in North Tulsa.

According to Burchard:

"He stood among his people - a three-piece suited crowd of lawyers, doctors, clothiers and druggists, owners of cafes, a hotel, night clubs, movie houses, dress shops, a newspaper, and general stores and grocery stores ."

Dr. Carver's last visit to Tulsa and Greenwood was in 1929 when he came to the dedication of the George Washington Carver Junior High School in early May. As on his previous visit, Carver stayed with my great-grandparents, J. H., and Carlie Goodwin.

My grandfather, E. L. Goodwin, Sr., and my grandmother Jeanne Goodwin lived next door to my great grandparents.

My grandfather worked in real estate with his dad and had several entrepreneurial investments.

My grandmother was teaching school at Booker T. Washington High School.

My grandmother would later say of Carver, "He didn't make you feel you were bothering him. It was in his nature to be courteous. But you knew he had better things to do than small talk. It was like he was in another world, looking forward or searching."

For the dedication ceremony, history records that over three thousand people from North and South Tulsa came out to hear Carver speak and enjoy naming a school for Black students after him. Afterward, Carver said having the school named after him was the most incredible honor he had ever received. On all accounts, Carver appeared visibly humbled by the dedication of this school to him.

By 1933, J. H. Goodwin's son, my grandfather E. L. Goodwin, Sr., had become a wealthy businessman.

After completing four years at Booker T. Washington High School, E. L. Goodwin, Sr., packed the trunk that his dad J. H. Goodwin had brought from Water Valley, Mississippi, to Tulsa, Oklahoma.

He boarded a train to Nashville, where he enrolled at Fisk University. Goodwin was a talented running back at Fisk, and the student body gave him the nickname "Sugar Man" for his sweet athletic feats on the Fisk gridiron. He came from a business family and, like his father, and in the philosophy of Booker T. Washington, he cast his bucket down as an entrepreneur after graduating from Fisk University.

E. L. Goodwin, Sr., was highly popular. The establishment mocked his political leadership in North Tulsa and what the white media considered were questionable business dealings. He earned the bulk of his money as the kingpin of Tulsa's "numbers" syndicate.

The "numbers" organization was the forerunner of the legalized Mega-Million and Powerball Lotteries now famous and run by 45 jurisdictions, plus the District of Columbia, Puerto Rico, and the Virgin Islands.

Playing the "numbers" was frowned upon in the early stages of the 20th century by the legal authorities. It was then, as it is today, gambling. I am sure E. L. Goodwin, Sr., would get a big laugh because, before the end of the 20th century, more than a third of the states would have a legalized numbers lottery.

Perhaps my grandfather was ahead of his time, a case of a business opportunity deemed illegal until the government figured out how it could be lucrative for them. In the fiscal year 2018, Americans spent $77.7 billion on lotteries, up from about $5 billion in 2017.

I feel the same about the marijuana industry, so many people are incarcerated for selling marijuana in the United States yet, it is legal to use for medical purposes in thirty-three states, the District of Columbia, and Puerto Rico, and totally legal in fifteen states.

Nevertheless, many people depended on the "numbers" to live their best life in early 20th century America, and E. L. Sr. used his earnings like a bank to fund other businesses in the area.

The white banks, now the only banks in town after Greenwood's demise, did not like this underground competition. The white media became an irritant to my grandfather. He understood the power of the press in influencing public opinion.

E. L., Sr., decided long before Rupert Murdock and Jeff Bezos that the best way to silence an editorial opinion that did not favor his business acumen was to own a medium of information and control the messaging.

In 1933, E. L., Sr. made an offer to buy the *Oklahoma Eagle* from Baughman. However, Baughman rejected his proposal on several occasions. Finally, in 1936, a year after my father was born, E. L., Sr., used his business savvy to gain the Oklahoma Eagle ownership.

He fronted a friend the money to invest in the newspaper. A year later, Baughman died, and my grandfather came into full ownership of the paper.

Edward L. Goodwin, Sr., bought the *Eagle* because he was tired of being vilified by the white Tulsa "metropolitan press." They disparagingly labeled him as "the black mayor of the City of Tulsa."

The white press did not like him, he said years later in an interview, "because I had become involved in all these illegal operations. So, the metropolitan press was so strong in their accusations against me, I said, 'Well, I guess this is a good thing for me to do. I'm going to buy one of these papers.'"

## "G-O-O-D-Y"

After a few months in the newspaper business, my grandfather understood the enormous power for good that a newspaper could fashion.

The *Eagle* became more than an instrument to create good press for him.

Within a few months in the publishing business, my grandfather realized that he could shape public opinion on the issues confronting the Black community. The masthead then and now reads: "We Make America, When We Aid Our People."

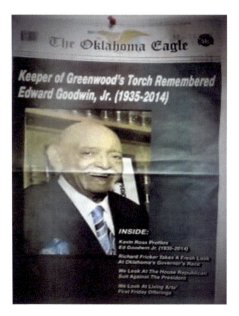

The headline of The Eagle announcing the transition of my father Edward "ED" Goodwin, Jr. Photo from *The Oklahoma Eagle.*

It became E. L., Sr.'s responsibility to bring the news into the homes of Black people in Tulsa and Oklahoma. My father, E. L. Jr., grew up at the *Oklahoma Eagle* office. He and his siblings worked at the *Eagle* for their father.

My grandfather believed in business ownership. He thought that a business was a family affair because everyone in the family benefited from the success of their business.

It came as no surprise that my father was able to work until shortly before he died. My father ate and slept in the newsrooms often.

He told the positive stories of Black people in Tulsa and other communities in Oklahoma from the pages of the Eagle, the Indianapolis Voice, the Kansas City Star, Tulsa Daily World, Sand Springs Leader, The Joplin Globe, and Daily Globe.

He would work for the newspapers at various stages of his lengthy journalism career.

He was truly a newspaperman.

E. L. Jr. had a grasp of the English language that escaped the grip of most Americans. He was fond of words and expertly rolled them off his tongue in spellbinding stories he told throughout his lifetime. He was known to use trenchant metaphors to point out ironies during political discourse. Like most veteran newspaper journalists, my father never retired. He always had his camera with him, and if he saw an event that needed amplification, he would take out his camera and tell the story.

Much of his story and the stories of pioneers of "The Negro Wall Street" were forged doing business in North Tulsa. This great American business district like "Sweet Auburn" in Atlanta, Georgia, but for the race massacre of 1921, would have thrived up to 1947.

Like "Sweet Auburn" the Greenwood area was later rebuilt and endures, albeit barely today. The year 1947 was signified by Jackie Robinson breaking the color barrier in baseball and setting America on a course correction where white-only spaces became occupied by Black Americans.

The Greenwood area was rebuilt after the 1921 race massacre and remained a stronghold in North Tulsa until Urban Renewal (Urban Removal) devastated the site in the mid-70s. This plot was played out in several urban areas throughout the United States.

Ten years before I was born in Cherryvale, Kansas, Jackie Robinson broke the color barrier in professional baseball.

That year, Oklahoma celebrated its 40th anniversary as the 46th state in the country.

During its first forty years as a state, no Black American had played on a team in the White Major Leagues. On April 15, 1947, that all changed when Jackie Robinson stepped onto the turf at Ebbets Field with his white Brooklyn Dodger teammates.

This singular event, I believe, set the tone for the most progress made in America since the terrible race massacre of 1921. Don't get me wrong; I am not taking anything away from the importance of the *Brown v. The Topeka Board of Education* decisions in 1954 and 1955, the 1964 Civil Rights Act, or the 1965 Voter Rights Act.

These court rulings and laws codified rights denied to Black Americans, but in 1947, placing Jackie Robinson on a Major League diamond prophetically embodied the spirit of the rules that were to come. I often argue the signing of Jackie Robinson was done more for economic gains than for racial equality. The Negro Leagues were thriving big time during the signing of Jackie Robinson.

Growing up, when Robinson broke into the major leagues, it affected generations yet unborn, like in my case. Baseball was such a big part of the Black community that I wanted to be a professional baseball player almost from the day I came into the world.

Sports seemed to transcend race and political differences then as it does today. He remains one of all-time favorite baseball player.

Because Black America was excited that a Black man was playing in the White professional league, baseball is the only sport adults talked about day and night.

By the time I came along, other Black players were playing with White baseball players. I especially liked Willie "The Say Hey Kid" Mays. He played with a flash and a flare and so much energy. Mr. Mays remains my favorite baseball player still today.

When baseball season was in, I followed the exploits of my favorite players daily. I knew their batting averages and could recite them to anyone who cared to listen. Mostly, my family grew tired of me repeating the various batting averages, runs batted in, and stolen bases.

Baseball and education have been my bridge into race relations and where I found my most fantastic avenue to public service as an adult. When I was about nine years old, an incident occurred in Little League baseball in Cherryvale, Kansas, that would help inform my thinking about race and public service.

As I stated earlier, I spent the first three years of my life in Cherryvale residing at my maternal grandparents' home. My dad worked in Tulsa, helping my grandfather run the *Oklahoma Eagle* and would travel the 88 miles to Cherryvale each weekend.

According to my Aunt, JoAnn Goodwin Gilford, educators identified my mom and dad as exceptional people.

In those early years living in Cherryvale, I would wait on the front steps for my uncle Jerry Parker, my mom's younger brother, to come home from work. He did not have a car at the time, and he walked home from work.

My brother Eric, an older cousin Barry, and I would sit on the front steps when we thought he should arrive home from work. My uncle Jerry was a good athlete. He played all the sports in high school: football, basketball, baseball, and track. He would be excited to play catch with us when he got home. We played baseball until it was too dark to see the ball.

Uncle Jerry would be excited – or at least he pretended excitement – to play catch with us when he got home. I'm sure as a young man he had other things to do. These games of catch would be my initial introduction to the game of baseball, a game I still love and encourage others to participate in because it provides so many life lessons.

Eventually, my father moved the family to Tulsa. I would spend the summer months in Cherryvale with my mother's parents, Harold Parker, Sr., and Bethel Bean Parker at 229 East 7th Street.

There was a lot of love in that house. The Parkers were a praying family, and a great deal of my demeanor comes from the patient instructions I received in the Parker home during my summer visits. My maternal grandma was a homemaker.

She did not work outside the home, so the duty of disciplining the grandchildren fell on her shoulders in the Parker family.

If she believed one of the grandchildren needed to learn a lesson the hard way, she would command that child to bring her a "switch," from the nearest tree, and school was in session.

I never felt her discipline was abusive because she was so loving. The fact that I had disappointed her by my behavior hurt worse than the few licks across my buttocks.

My granddad, on my mother's side, was a quiet man. He spoke when he thought it necessary. He did not waste words, nor did he mince them when it was time to tell someone what was really on his mind. We revered granddad.

Granddad Parker had two jobs, one full-time and one part-time. Five days a week, he drove to Coffeyville, Kansas, where he worked as a smithy. Granddad Parker forged iron and other metals at the Ozark Smithering and Mining Company. He was a skilled craftsman.

We would sit on the back steps late in the afternoon, waiting for his car to drive up. Before Granddad could get out of the car, we would run to the car and help him with his lunch box. He always left a treat in his lunch box for us to discover when he got home from work. His part-time hustle was as the janitor at a utility company that supplied gas to residential and commercial businesses in Cherryvale.

On this job, he cleaned up the offices after they closed for the day. He was a hardworking, no-nonsense man who provided for his family.

As the grandchildren got older, we got to help granddad at the evening job at the gas company office.

He enjoyed watching *Gunsmoke* on the television. When Gunsmoke came on, you could hear a pin drop in the house. We knew not to be loud nor distract him when his favorite program was on.

The quickest way to get on his wrong side was to talk over the television when he watched Matt Dillion take care of business in Dodge City, Kansas.

I still watch reruns of Gunsmoke! The reruns never get old.

During the summer months when I was in Cherryvale, I would get up early and go fishing. I loved to fish. I was rather good at it. My grandma would cook the fish that I brought back from my fishing excursions at Lake Tanko.

My older cousin Barry showed my brother Eric and I the ropes during those summers in Cherryvale. Barry was like an older brother.

Grandma Parker taught us a valuable lesson about waste from outings at the pond. Once we caught a batch of small fish and threw them back into the water. My grandma said that everything had some utility, and I should bring them all home and figure out how to use them.

This lecture was a simple lesson in "waste not, want not."

In the afternoons, I would go out and play sandlot baseball with my friends. We generally had several games per week. These were usually afternoon games. We would participate in the neighborhood games until the little league season began.

As far back as I can remember, I have always loved baseball. When I was a toddler, the family lore says that Willie Mays would flow off my tongue as often as I would say, mama and daddy.

From R-L Eric Goodwin, Barry Vick, Greg Goodwin, Sherry Vick, Regina Goodwin sitting in Sherry's lap, Sabrina Goodwin Monday, and Michelle Mason, (family of siblings and cousins) in the living room of the family home at 1415 North Greenwood Street, Tulsa, Oklahoma. Photo from the Goodwin collection.

I can't explain it. There is something about the game that I just love. Still today, I am happiest when I am around a baseball diamond, especially when teaching baseball and the game of life to young people.

I played youth league baseball in Cherryvale. I was the only Black kid in the league at the time. My uncles, cousin, and brother had played in the local Little League before I participated.

In the beginning, it wasn't a big deal. I blended in with my White teammates. I was having fun playing my favorite sport.

Each year after school let out for the summer, my parents dropped my siblings and I off at my maternal grandparents' home. My aunts and uncles did the same with their children. Cherryvale would be our summer resort.

My grandparents would register me to play on the Little League team in the community. The guys on my team never considered that I was Black - at least it was never discussed - we resumed the pickup games that we played daily at the *Majewski's lot* until league play. We played together and had fun.

On game days, my granddad would drive me to the game. The field made it possible for him and grandma to sit in the car and watch the game. Sometimes he would sit on the hood of his car. He never sat in the stands, as did some parents of my teammates.

It did not dawn on me why my granddad did not sit in the bleachers with the other parents. I never asked them, as other white parents sat in cars as well.

But as an adult, I did ask my Uncle Jerry, and he assured me that parents and guardians would arrive at the park early to get good parking spots so they could blow the horns from the cars. They could show their approval of a timely hit or a stellar defensive play.

In Cherryvale, there were no segregated facilities for White and Black people like in Tulsa. My mom attended school with White kids and gave no thought to it.

My dad's experience growing up in Tulsa was the direct opposite. Separation was the order of the day. Please understand, this was due more to economics than equal rights. Many of my aunts and uncles on my mom's side were the only Black in their classes.

Whenever we did something good in the game, grandad would honk the car horn to let us know that he supported what we were accomplishing on the field. I loved to hear his car horn blasting over the park because it meant that my granddad was proud of me.

At the end of each summer, we played a tournament to crown the city champion. For a couple of years, the team I was on came close to reaching the championship game. We always came up short.

Then one year, we won all our games in the championship tournament and made it to the championship game.

In my first at-bat during the championship game, I hit a double off the fence. Above the crowd's roar, I could hear my granddad's car horn, and I was feeling good all over as I stood at second base. The guys were shouting; my teammates were soaking it in. Our chances of winning the championship looked good.

I was floating on a cloud of excitement. Then suddenly, the roar of the crowd hushed as a White man approached me at second base.

As he came closer, I recognized him as the president of the league. He walked out to the second base and told me I was suspended and could not play in the game.

Before I knew it, my grandad had left his car and was standing on the field, engaging the league president in a conversation. It was the first time he had left his car to walk onto the field and interact with anyone else at the ballpark.

Hearing that his grandson received a suspension for hitting a ball to the fence brought him onto the field that day. The president said that I was ineligible to play because I did not reside in Cherryvale year round.

In none of the previous years had anyone objected to me playing in the Cherryvale Little League program. The whole town knew that I was in town each summer visiting with my grandparents and that I would return to Tulsa at the end of the summer.

We did not hide the fact that I did not live year-round in Cherryvale.

When I hit that double in the championship game, suddenly, I was an ineligible player.

I was unaware of the social mores of the times. In retrospect, my grandparents were aware of them. Race relations were not a big deal in Cherryvale. At least not until a Black kid might lead his team to a City Championship.

The league president knew the ways of the southwest very well. He would not allow a team with a Black player to win the city championship if he could help it; he could help the situation by disqualifying the heavy-hitting Black player before the game got out of reach of the all-white local team.

The suspension was my first personal glimpse that all was not well in America. I did not understand it. I knew that something was wrong when White people had rules for White people and different rules for Black people when Blacks outperformed White people. It would never happen in Tulsa because I was playing in a segregated environment in the Tulsa Little Leagues.

What happened next has filled me with pride to this very day. My family members showed up at the ballpark and protested my suspension from the tournament.

By Saturday of the next week, a contingent of relatives as far away as Denver, Colorado ascended on downtown Cherryvale to stage a protest in front of the business (a men's clothing store) of the league's president.

The protest had the tiny town of Cherryvale shook up. According to the 1960 census, Cherryvale only had 3,206 residents. Most of them were White. So, Black people did not draw attention to themselves. They went quietly about town; however, they were very active in school and town events.

Black protest simply did not happen in Cherryvale. For the small Black population in Cherryvale, suspending me in the middle of a championship baseball game was an injustice that rubbed them the wrong way; and we had to resist it. Racism and prejudices had not been on public display in Cherryvale, as far as I knew.

Generally, the races got along together, so when the league commissioner ruled me ineligible for the championship game after I had nearly hit the ball out of the ballpark, it just did not feel right. Everybody knew that his actions came from a very dark place.

The whole town took notice of the Parker and Goodwin family protest. Shortly after the demonstrations, the summer ended, the ruling remained, I returned to school in Tulsa. We didn't win that battle, but I learned a valuable lesson.

For several weeks afterward, I walked down the hallways with my chest stuck out. I did not understand why at the time, but I knew we had done something good. When I returned to Cherryvale the following summer, there was no problem with me playing in the youth league.

My uniform was waiting for me. The league president understood his business needed Cherryvale Blacks to patronize his business for him to be successful.

As I have explained before I was the only Black on the team and my grandparents were well respected. They had several White friends that would have boycotted the clothing store as well.

The people of Cherryvale did not know they were messing with a descendant of J. H. Goodwin, Sr, a man who had survived the Tulsa Race Massacre of 1921 with grit and professional manners.

Cherryvale already knew about the Parkers as my granddad's nickname was "Bear" in the Cherryvale community. They were quickly reminded not to wake "The Bear," that the kindness of the Parker family could turn on a dime if a member of the family received mistreatment. We eventually won that war.

# Part TWO
# Greenwood

My life in Tulsa was the life of a typical boy who lived in an entrepreneurial family.

My father was a newspaperman. His father was a newspaperman, and because they owned their printing press, I became immersed in the newspaper business.

Everyone in my family worked in the newspaper office. Daddy had three older sisters, Oneatha, Edwyna, and JoAnn, two younger brothers, Jim, and Bob, and three younger sisters, Jeanne, Carlye, and Susan.

They, too, were instrumental in preparing me for life. I was so fortunate to be surrounded by two loving families.

After my last sibling, Regina started school, mama joined my daddy at the *Oklahoma Eagle*, keeping the books and running the business.

I learned all aspects of the newspaper business, from editorial to production to circulation. Putting a newspaper together is intense but rewarding work.

After writing the stories that would be in the newspaper, daddy would operate the printing press.

A newspaperman's newspaperman, Ed Goodwin reading a fresh off the press edition of the *Oklahoma Eagle*. Photo from the Goodwin collection.

Black ink from the printing press covered him on press days. On the day we put the newspaper to bed, we would not leave the newspaper office until around 2:00 a. m., sometimes later, if we had problems with the printing press.

I was a teenager and received promotions several times when I was assigned these late duties. I would not receive any pay raises but took great pride in giving myself a new title. I was a genius at self-promotion.

When I was in the second grade, and the papers came off the press, I received a promotion from taking out trash cans and cleaning the bathroom to paperboy. I liked the upgrade because I did not get paid to empty the trash or clean the bathrooms.

As a paperboy, I got paid to sell the papers, my first paid job. The newspapers sold for ten cents apiece. I learned about money selling the newspaper. I knew that if a person worked hard, you could make money.

The *Eagle* hired other kids in the community to sell the papers, but my brother and I would get our newspapers as soon as they came off the press because we were family. The other guys would be lined up at the door to get their papers. We would go up and down Greenwood Avenue selling the newspapers.

It was an easy product to sell because everybody in North Tulsa could not wait to get the new edition of the local weekly when it hit the street. Remember, this was the 1960s. The *Eagle* was our voice which carried our news. There were no computers, no social media, no cell phones, just print media, and man, was it our news. My brother Eric and I always had a head start on the other carriers.

Additionally, the newspaper boy job taught me that a bit of business savvy was having and taking advantage of opportunities that the competition did not have.

I would hit the local barbershops, beauty shops, restaurants, and pool halls, as they were full of individuals willing to spend a dime with a kid.

My daddy had a good compensation package for the other kids to make up for the time advantage practically living in the paper gave us. Dad would pay the other boys five cents out of every newspaper they sold, a whopping 50 percent profit. A kid could buy a lot of bubble gum with baseball trading cards at those rates.

From the time I was able to go to the *Eagle* office, I was sitting in various meetings like production, editorial, circulation, and advertisement.

I was privy to every business discussion that took place at the *Eagle*. They had about 20 employees on the payroll. It did not take me long to realize that the sale of the papers did not bring in enough money to pay the staff.

Then I got an education in marketing, promotion, and advertising.

I learned to market by watching my daddy, Lee Turpin, Elmer Davis, Sr., and Uncle Bob market the newspaper.

After another disagreement between my grandfather and my dad, the family patriarch summoned Uncle Bob back from California to take over the newspaper. Daddy's struggles with alcoholism didn't help in his attempt to run the weekly newspaper. It was a blessing that he eventually gave up both drinking and smoking.

Weekly, we sold the *Eagle* in every grocery store, barbeque joint, café, and barbershop on Greenwood. These customer service skills have served me well in every industry where I have worked. I eventually worked my way up to what was labeled running the route. The route was given to a relative who had a driver's license and that was lucrative for a teenager.

Around eleven or twelve years of age, I was assigned duties related to the circulation department. I learned how to use the tying machine to bundle newspapers that we shipped to out of town subscribers.

We had a large circulation throughout the United States and shipped a sizable number of papers each week to other cities in the country (They still do).

We worked without pay. I did not feel anything about not getting paid for the work I did at the newspaper office. It was the way it was. I had free room and board and clean clothes daily, so I did get paid in that sense. I never lacked for anything.

Everyone in the family was responsible for ensuring that the business was successful, and I was happy to do my part. The family never denied me when I needed to purchase new cleats or gym shoes to continue my athletic pursuits.

But when I became 15 years old, my dad allowed my brother and me to take the aluminum printing plates to the recyclable yard where we would sell them.

I liked this job the best because we could keep the money we earned from selling the aluminum plates. I had just gotten my driver's license, and the money came in handy for walking around change, movies, and dating. Grandfather, Daddy, and Uncle Bob had this way about them. They would find unique ways to reward you after a period of working for nothing.

I crossed the railroad track and ventured into South Tulsa when I turned 14 in order to earn more money and took a job at a McDonald's franchise making $1.60 an hour. Putting this wage into perspective, in 1957, when I was born, the national minimum wage was $1.00.

There were no McDonald franchises in North Tulsa in 1971.

It was the early 1970s, a time of unbelievable change. I was happy with that job. I had an opportunity to work with one of my best childhood friends, Lester Shaw, and we had fun. Too much fun. We probably should have been fired. Dr. Shaw and I remain good friends today.

About this time, my grandfather, Edward Goodwin, Sr., decided he was going into the catfish farming business. He dedicated a piece of land he owned in Alsuma, Oklahoma, to developing a state-of-the-art catfish farm.

Alsuma was a small township outside of Tulsa that Blacks inhabited, beginning in the 1900s when Alsuma was in Indian Territory. It had its own post office and a school for the education of Black children. My grandmother taught in this school. Alsuma mainly was a Black community, and there were Whites in the town.

Like Tulsa, the two communities were separated by a railroad track, except for a White family that lived across the street from Grandfather's property. I am not sure when my granddad bought this piece of property. He had held it for a long time before he decided to live on the property during the mid-1940s when he moved his family from North Tulsa to Alsuma.

There was a big house on the property, and he renovated it to accommodate his family. The property came with a pond. I enjoyed going out to Alsuma to visit with my grandparents. Grandfather was different from most people you meet.

He loved life and making money. He once owned a nightclub named "The *Goody - Goody*." He had lots of chickens, guinea fowl, turkeys, and peacocks roaming around the property.

My grandfather was a well-educated and well-rounded man. He finished Tulsa University Law School in his 50s. He shared with me that one of the things he noticed was he spent quite a bit of money on lawyers.

He thought about how much money he could save with a law degree, so he enrolled in law school and became a lawyer.

After raising his family, while successfully publishing a weekly newspaper and practicing law, grandfather decided to develop five additional ponds on the Alsuma property to begin his final business venture, Goodwin Catfish Farm.

He stocked the ponds with Channel Catfish. People would come from Tulsa and surrounding towns to fish.

They paid a fee to fish in the catfish ponds. Also, they would pay a fee per pound for the catfish they caught.

He was getting up in age and came to recruit me to help him operate the catfish farm. I was young and strong and eager to learn new things.

Initially, I balked at joining the family catfish farm. The job at McDonald's paid me a whopping buck sixty, and I was having so much fun on the job with my friend Lester Shaw that the time spent at McDonald's did not seem like work.

But grandfather was persistent. He told me that I had a better chance of owning the catfish farm one day than owning a McDonald's franchise. It was a common-sense decision, but I have learned that common sense is far from common.

In 1972 there was no way to deny the truth of his argument. Also, the money I could make working on the catfish farm would give me an enormous nest egg to take to college, or so I was led to believe. His idea was logical and made a whole lot of sense.

So, I quit my job at McDonald's and started ripping and running on the catfish farm. My grandfather told me that he would turn the catfish farm over to me when he retired.

Everything he told me to do, I did it. I worked my butt off. We had four ponds that we kept stocked with catfish and another pond where we kept the fingerlings (smaller fish).

The public could come in and fish. I made good money cleaning channel catfish for customers who did not want to clean the fish they caught.

In the beginning, we were doing well. Grandfather knew a wholesaler in Oklahoma City. We ordered truckloads of catfish from this wholesaler. Then one day, I was out in the boat with my grandfather trying to fix an aerator in the back pond.

We were dressed that day in our heavy fishing boots and work clothing. Grandfather stood up, and the boat began to tilt to one side. I told him that he should sit down before the boat flipped. He did not hear me, or he ignored me, which was a common practice of his. In any event, he did not sit down.

Suddenly the boat capsized and threw us into the water. I was an avid swimmer, but my grandfather began to panic even though he could swim.

I saw him fighting in the water and went to help him get back inside the boat. He began to fight me. But I would not give up. There was no way I was going to let my grandfather drown. Each time I thought I had him under control, he would push my head under the water as he fought to get out of the water.

Finally, I could swim with my grandfather under my arm and made it back onshore. I had just saved my grandfather's life; heart-pounding, adrenaline rushing over me, grandfather began to accuse me of trying to drown him.

He called me some of the worst names imaginable. He did not accept responsibility for flipping the boat or pulling me back into the water as I struggled to save his life. He could have caused both of us to drown that day.

Trust me, this is the truth, but it is not how grandfather told the story. We were both fortunate to have an opportunity to tell our version of the story. I promise had he still been living; I would not have included this story in this book. He was a loving man but could also be quite intimidating.

The veil lifted; I had been so naïve to think that the catfish farm would belong to me one day. When my grandfather filled me with the pipe dream of owning the catfish farm, I did not know about deeds and how property is distributed during probate when a person dies.

My grandfather had a wife and several children in the line of succession to receive a piece of his 160 acres before it would come to me. I was not thinking that all the children would go out on their own and would have little interest in maintaining a farm of 160 acres.

I set my eyes on owning my own business. I was briefly disappointed when I snapped out of my grandfather's pipe dream.

In retrospect, had the events of that day never happened, I probably would not have left Tulsa. All the experiences I have lived, the lives I have touched and changed for the better, would not have materialized.

With the energy I put into the things I am involved in; we probably would be selling catfish worldwide. In all seriousness, I can never thank both sets of my grandparents for pouring good precepts and examples into all their grandchildren, including me.

I am grateful for two tough, real men.
Also two gracious, humble God-fearing women.

They were great, awesome grandparents who I was blessed to have for a good part of my life.

At other times growing up, I would tag along with daddy as he went throughout Tulsa to cover the news.

Exciting people were constantly dropping by the newsroom to talk with my daddy. At other times, I would go to events in Tulsa with my daddy.

I met many of the influential people of the last half of the 20th century. I met Muhammad Ali, Ralph J. Bunche, Moms Mabley, James Brown, you name them; if they came to Tulsa, my daddy would make sure that his family got to meet them. I met Martin Luther King, Jr. on a visit to Tulsa, tagging along with my dad.

When I was about eleven or twelve, I found that I could defuse a potentially volatile situation with humor. I was at the airport with my daddy to meet a celebrity that dad planned to interview. While waiting for the plane to arrive, I got bored and asked him if I could look around in the gift shop. He said it was okay.

The flight arrived later than expected. I spent about an hour looking at all the merchandise on display in the gift shop.

A police officer approached me and asked what I was doing in the gift shop. I told him I was looking around. But my answer did not satisfy the officer. He followed that question by asking, "Boy, have you ever been in trouble."

My quick-witted mind retorted, "Yes, there was this time when my baseball team had tied the game in the ninth inning with the bases loaded, and I was at the bat. Mister, now that's big trouble."

I wanted to burst out laughing, but the officer grew red in the face indicating he did not find me amusing with my glib remark. My dad strolled into the gift shop to get me by that time, and the officer had to leave me alone.

My dad taught me that you could say whatever you want when you are right. I have carried that lesson with me my entire life. Those who know me will also share that humor and laughter is a huge part of my life.

Greg "Goody" Goodwin and Edward "Goody" Goodwin October 19, 2012. Photo from the Goodwin collection.

One day, Dr. Martin Luther King, Jr. came to Tulsa to speak at First Baptist Church of North Tulsa; the church was and still is located at 1414 North Greenwood, across the street from the house where Urban Renewal forced us to move out of the home house. My father took us to hear him speak. I was about seven years old. I did not understand the magnitude of who he was, but I could tell he was an important man and that many people respected him.

A few years later, when someone assassinated Dr. King in Memphis, Tennessee, I was at home watching the television with the family when the announcement came on the television that an assassin had killed Dr. King.

I was 10 years old and a fifth-grade student at Burroughs Elementary School. I thought about the day my dad took me to hear Dr. King speak. Then I took out my pen and wrote a poem titled Martin Luther King:

*Martin Luther, a name to remember,*
*As everyone called him Mister and Sir,*
*A friend to everyone,*
*I doubt if he owned a gun,*
*A shot rang out like a sudden shout,*
*And there on the tower with all his*
*Power and pride, he died,*
*So I say once more, Martin Luther King,*

## "G-O-O-D-Y"

*A name to remember as everyone called him Mister and sir.*

> This poem was published in the Oklahoma Eagle on April 11, 1968, two days after Dr. King's memorial service in Atlanta, Georgia.

My father packed up his camera five days after King's assassination and headed to Atlanta to cover Dr. King's funeral for the *Eagle*. In the edition of the *Eagle* where my poem appeared, Stokely Carmichael's quote: "White America made its biggest mistake when she killed Dr. King. She killed all reasonable hope."

When Daddy introduced a celebrity to you, it was like introducing you to an old friend. Many times, it would be the first time that he had met that personality too.

Daddy treated everybody the same, no matter their walk of life; I thought these great men and women were just ordinary people, which they probably were. Daddy's manner of introducing famous people taught me not to be in awe of the people I met; after all, they are just ordinary people like me.

If I had to put my finger on the one thing Daddy taught me that had molded me into the person I am today, I would say it was watching him treat everybody the same. He would spend the same time greeting sanitation workers and street sweepers as doctors, lawyers, and preachers.

Daddy would take immense pride in reciting the Rudyard Kipling poem, "If," which includes the words, *"If you can talk with crowds and keep your virtue Or walk with Kings and keep the common touch. Yours is the earth and everything in it, and – which is more – you'll be a Man, my son."*

I must have heard him recite it a million times.

Both parents taught me that everybody in life should receive equal treatment.

My mother was a stickler for proper pronunciation and respecting elders.

I'm 65 years of age and still say yes sir or yes mam to anyone I believe might be over 40. Everybody has worth, and everybody has importance.

When I was a principal, I empowered the custodians to the extent that if they had cleaned an area and saw a student mess it up, they had the authority to correct them.

I believed that was showing respect to the janitor. This helped me communicate the importance of treating everybody in the community with respect, no matter their station in life.

This essential lesson has been crucial to my success as an adult servant leader. I owe this lesson to my parents.

My mom explained the importance of having good manners, respecting our elders, and the value of an education. Mama did not play when it came to school.

She preached making good grades and not getting into trouble whatever you do. Mama knew the Goodwin and the Parker names had a long and rich history in Tulsa and Cherryvale. Also, she knew that my siblings and I owed our ancestors an obligation to uphold the family reputation started by J. H. Goodwin, Sr., and Alfred Parker (my granddad's father) in the early 20th century.

The Parkers didn't play either. We certainly were not allowed to misbehave while in Cherryvale. To make sure no one gets it twisted, my siblings and I learned about "weblo's" early from the Parkers.

"Weblo" is a swift cup or tap at the back of your head at the first sign of any misbehaving. We do a "weblo" ceremony for new additions to the family at the Parker family gatherings. Fun and laughter, and a steady diet of working hard, was a staple we received from both sides of the family.

When I look at the two parents the "Good Lord" gave me, I have to say; that I hit the lottery. They were strict but fair. They taught me to be independent, carry my load, and work in a group.

Their lessons have made me the person that I am. When people give me accolades, all I can say is that I would not be in this position to hear these kind words directed toward me but for my parents and the extraordinary village that helped raise me.

I enrolled in the famous Booker T. Washington High School when I began high school.

I later became a third-generation Booker T. Washington High graduate, graduating in the remarkable class of 1975.

I am no doubt blessed to have many close friends from my childhood. The same school where my grandfather was the night of the Tulsa Race Massacre in 1921.

He and his classmates were preparing for the senior prom when word reached the school that roaming bands of armed White men threatened to cross the railroad tracks into North Tulsa.

Adults in my community did not talk about the Tulsa Race Massacre during my childhood. My daddy taught me what he could remember from what he learned from his dad. However, generations past have essentially shut the memory of this horrible atrocity out of their minds. Community leaders did not pass much information about it to their children.

On reflection: who could blame folks for not speaking of this tragedy. The North Tulsa community was nurturing and vibrant despite its tragic history.

Perhaps, their resilience is the lesson the people of North Tulsa taught the world.

"It's not what you do to me," history seems to record, "it's how I overcome it."

My grandmother Jeanne Goodwin often told us to be better, not bitter.

Growing up in my parent's home and newspaper office, I was always around reading material. There were newspapers, of course, and books and magazines that came to the newspaper. Every month a new *Ebony Magazine* floated into the house, and every week *Jet Magazine* came in the mail. I would read these magazines and dream of a world outside of Tulsa.

The Greenwood area was a majestic neighborhood.

My friends Eddie Gill, Kenneth Jones, Melvin Barrens, the King Boys, the Grundy's, Marvin Foster, Michael Johnson, Theopolis Duhart, Reggie Midget, Hooks, Jupiter, Kerrye Woods, Greg Walker, and many more, kept things exciting.

I especially liked the *Jet Magazine*. I developed an interest in Tennessee State University from the pages of Jet. *Jet's* stories about the Tennessee State football team and Head Football Coach John Merritt, their world-class Olympic track athletes like Wilma Rudolph, Ralph Boston, and their magnificent band would have me mesmerized.

Without a doubt, I wanted to be a Tennessee State University Tiger when I grew up. Schools recognized my ability on the baseball field in Tulsa. I had a few scholarships, but none from Tennessee State University, so I wrote the baseball coach.

He wrote back and informed me that he did not recruit that far away from the state of Tennessee, but if I enrolled in the school, I was welcome to try out for the team. That is all I needed to hear. My heart which had bled Booker T. Washington Hornet orange slowly started to turn Tennessee State University Tiger blue.

## "G-O-O-D-Y"

In my junior year of high school, I was elected the junior class president and selected to the All-City baseball team. I was elected the senior class president and captain of the baseball team in my senior year. These two offices enabled me to develop my leadership style and skills. My mama was pleased with my educational achievement but consistently reminded me that I could do better.

She also knew when I would lose focus and would quickly get me back on track. Education was her "Big Thing." She expected each of her children to hit the books hard. And I hit the books and the baseball hard during my high school years. I never played summer baseball in high school. I was busy working one of my several jobs.

My years of high school were challenging school years. To begin with, eighteen years after the Supreme Court ruled in *Brown v. The Topeka Board of Education*, school systems should use all "deliberate speed" in desegregating public schools in America, the Tulsa County Board of Education integrated the school system in Tulsa. So much for deliberate speed.

Before the Tulsa County Board of Education got around to integrating the public schools, my aunt, Jo-Ann Goodwin Gilford integrated the teaching faculty at

John Burroughs Elementary School in 1961. That year she was 28 years old and just back from Germany, where she had taught children of military servicemen, both Black and White. The Tulsa County Board of Education looked for a Black teacher to teach White children, and Aunt JoAnn met the requirement.

But even at 28 years of age and having lived in Europe, she was afraid to venture into the segregated Tulsa Public School System alone. She asked her father, my grandfather, to go with her to the interview. Together they walked into a heretofore segregated area of Tulsa. She received the job and accepted it. The school was primarily White.

A few years later, I enrolled in the first grade at Burroughs. Soon most of the White kids left the school. Only a few who could not afford private school tuition remained or whose parents could not afford to move.

Initially in 1972, the Tulsa County Board of Education attempted to close the historic Booker T. Washington High School, but the community pushback was so strong the board abandoned that idea.

Closing Booker T. Washington High School to accommodate desegregation was a socioreligious act. If the board of education did not realize that fact, the descendants of the rich legacy of Booker T. Washington High would let them know that the school was hallowed ground for the people of North Tulsa. We would not allow Whites in South Tulsa to shut down our high school because Booker T. had been the road to affluence for many people in North Tulsa.

A large book, no doubt, can be written about the number of influential African Americans who graduated from Booker T. Washington High School in Tulsa, Oklahoma, before integration. These women and men have achieved greatness in every field of endeavor. I was blessed to have several of these North Tulsa icons as mentors.

Julius Pegues, among others, was an activist who championed our cause. I tried to assure him of his importance to the greater Tulsa community and to me often during his larger-than-life existence.

Mr. Pegues transitioned March 29, 2022. He and dad were best friends.

Also, Mr. Pegues graduated from Booker T. Washington High School, class of 1953. He was the class valedictorian and attended the University of Pittsburgh.

Mr. Pegues walked onto the basketball team and earned a full scholarship after his performance in the first three games. He was the thirty-first pick of the St.

Louis Hawks of the National Basketball Association in 1957.

But rejected their offer for a career in engineering after obtaining a degree in Mechanical Engineering. Mr. Pegues served as my mentor until his death.

The Board did not realize or care how deep the ties of Booker T. Washington High School were in the Black community of North Tulsa. The school opened in 1913, two years before the death of Booker T. Washington.

Greg "Goody" Goodwin dancing with Aunt JoAnn.
Photo from the Goodwin collection.

It was unheard of in the early 20th century to name a building after a living person.

The Black community named the school after Booker T. Washington despite him being alive and well in 1913, demonstrating how revered Washington was in the North Tulsa community.

After all, Booker T. Washington High had survived the fires of the 1921 Tulsa Race Massacre. After which, the Red Cross set up relief operations in the school.

If the Board dismantled this leading symbol of Black progress in North Tulsa, the Black community would have none. Booker T. Washington High was the crown jewel of North Tulsa.

The Board devised a plan for 500 white volunteer students to attend Booker T. Washington High School and 500 Black students to attend the local high school.

This plan was developed by a North Tulsa icon and one of my mentors, Mr. Julius Pegues. He shared with me that we didn't have other options to save our school.

In several other Black communities, the desegregation of the public school system meant closing the Black school and busing all Black students to the White schools. The opposite was the case in Tulsa. The White kids volunteered to attend Booker T. Washington High, while over half of the Black students who had previously attended our beloved Booker T. Washington High would be forced, without a choice, to ride buses to the White High Schools.

The Tulsa plan sent Granville Smith, the Black principal at Booker T. Washington High, to Nathan

Hale, one of the White schools. The White principal, H. J. Green at Hale became the principal at Booker T.

In 1974, my brother Eric served as the first black student government president at Nathan Hale after being suspended and ultimately transferring there from Booker T. Washington. But this is another story for another book.

Like most members of the Goodwin family, Eric was a people person. In 1973 he met a White kid from South Tulsa named William "Bill" Padek, in the theater, at Booker T. Washington High.

Bill visited Booker T. Washington to decide if he would transfer from Nathan Hale High School to Booker T. Washington in Tulsa's first effort to integrate its segregated school system.

When Padek strolled into the theater, he saw a tall Black kid who greeted him with an outstretched hand. Other than the two maids his mother employed; this was the first Black person Padek had met personally.

That Black kid was Eric; the two teenagers became inseparable friends for the rest of Eric's time on earth. Eric would succumb to injuries from a car wreck as a young man in 1987.

Padek was thrilled to meet Eric, and this chance meeting helped him transfer to Booker T. Washington. Padek did not realize that his newfound friend had decided to transfer to Nathan Hale.

The two students introduced their circle of friends from their respective departing schools. Those introductions made it easy for them to enroll at their new schools.

Padek, one of the top pitchers in the Tulsa area, missed his baseball teammates at Nathan Hale High School by springtime. So he transferred back to Hale.

Years later, I told him how disappointed I was when he moved back to Hale because I looked forward to having him as my teammate on the Booker T. Washington baseball squad. We could have used his talented right arm at Booker T Washington. Padek moved on to attend Oklahoma State University and Eric to Howard, and their friendship continued.

## "G-O-O-D-Y"

Greg "Goody Goodwin, Alquita Goodwin (Mama), and Eric Goodwin are seated from left to right. Photo from the Goodwin collection.

Sometime after college Padek accepted a job offer in Houston, Texas. Eric lived there He worked on the staff of Congressman Mickey Leland. Padek did not know anyone in Houston except Eric and did not have any place to stay. He called Eric - problem solved - Eric invited him to move in with him.

Later, Padek's brother, Randy, received a job offer in Houston, and Eric solved his angst about where he would stay. Always looking out for others is the type of person Eric was the type of man dedicated to the service of others that our mama and daddy preached about to us every day. You were guaranteed a good time hanging with Eric. He was the proverbial "life of the party."

Years later, when Padek married, Eric was asked to be a groomsman. A snowstorm in Kansas City, the wedding site, prevented Eric from traveling to the ceremony from Houston.

Ironically, Padek and I married young ladies from Kansas City. Today, the Padeks and Goodwin families remain close friends.

Later, Eric Goodwin became the Chief of Staff for Coretta Scott King at the King Center for Non-Violence Social Change. Jesse Hill, a leading Black businessman in Atlanta at that time, said that Eric was responsible for shepherding the National Holiday for Dr. Martin Luther King, Jr. into law.

When Eric visited Mrs. King at the King residence, he was one of a few people who could sit in Dr. King's favorite chair. In the early morning hours of September 18, 1987, Eric was the victim of a fatal car accident.

Yolanda King, Dr. King's oldest child, spoke at his memorial service; my parents, my sisters Sabrina and

Regina, and myself, were devastated. Eric was only 31, a life well-lived.

Close family friends, and fellow civil rights activist friends of the family, Doris Crenshaw, and Kathy Nealy were strong and steady comforters during this very difficult time.

Eric transferred from Booker T. Washington in 1973.

Yet he forged relationships across racial lines and helped smooth the integration of Booker T. Washington High School.

Many Black students remaining at Booker T. Washington resented that our friends rode buses across town to other schools, even though they could have walked to Booker T. Washington.

It just wasn't right, but hey, who said life was fair?

Several Black students pushed back at the new kids who had enrolled in our school. There was not going to be a smooth transition. Many were not happy campers, and the White students knew it.

In the 1975 Yearbook, Connie Cole, Booker T.'s first White yearbook editor, sums up the precarious situation the White students found themselves in during the early days of school integration in Tulsa this way:

"We conformed at first so we could observe from the sidelines, then as we began to test the water a little.

We grew into individuals and made attempts at communication that we applauded ourselves for starting. But we got to the point of no return; we began to talk to each other thinking we understood."

There is no way, in my opinion, the White kids could understand Black students who remained at Booker T. Washington. We did not appreciate their angst either. All the Black adult leaders had always told us to stay on the North Tulsa side of the railroad track.

Being in an all-Black world is all we knew. Change is rarely easy.

We felt safe in our community, and because we had everything we wanted in North Tulsa, we did not feel as if we were missing anything segregated from Whites across the railroad track.

As far as most of us were concerned, the Whites could stay on their side of the railroad track, and it would not bother us or improve our situation one iota. After all, we were able to witness Black greatness daily in North Tulsa.

How could we miss what we had never experienced?

Our parents did not tell us why we should stay within the boundary of North Tulsa, other than it was safer than going across the tracks and getting into a physical altercation with a White person living in South Tulsa.

No one told us about the horrible Tulsa Race Massacre of 1921. I guess our parents and grandparents did not want to scare us, so they did not talk about the reign of terror visited upon North Tulsa by Whites from South Tulsa one hundred years ago.

I'm not sure our White classmates knew what their ancestors had done to our ancestors in the roaring 1920s.

I don't think White families talked about what had happened to instill pride into their children and grandchildren about the night their menfolk defended the honor of a White girl by burning down homes, hospitals, schools, hotels and murdering over 300 people in North Tulsa.

I am not naive enough to think racism is a thing of the past. I can only pray that things continue to get better. It was evident during the 2020 Presidential election that racial issues are still perverse in our country.

We cannot speculate about the motives of the integration of our beloved Booker T. Washington High. I remain grateful for the leaders of North Tulsa, including my mentor Mr. Julius Pegues, who served on committees to bring an amicable solution to the desegregation of the Tulsa Public School District.

Mr. Pegues is a legendary figure, not only for his athletic prowess but for his engineering professional accomplishments, and his leadership role in North Tulsa.

Like Black children, perhaps White kids my age did not know the harm done in their name a century ago. The White kids may not have known they had lived a privileged life where their ideas and desires had received little challenge in their White worldview.

In contrast, Black students had learned to be independent of White privilege by not venturing across the railroad tracks unless necessary.

Those necessities included working as maids and yardmen, as well as country club waiters.

Those travels were deemed appropriate. However, these workers were expected to be back in North Tulsa by sundown.

Whatever the case, the first White students did not come aggressively; they came seeking to unite with a new Booker T. Washington spirit.

While most of us, on the other hand, liked things just as they were. We were not used to social changes benefiting us. In fact had the White students not volunteered to integrate Booker T., who knows whether the school might have closed?

We liked that old Booker T. spirit just as it had been when our parents were students at the school. We were not so much against the White students.

Our fight was with the board of education to break up our friendships and send our friends across town to school.

Much of what I learned from my experiences as class president during my junior and senior years in high school would serve me well in my career: as a professional baseball scout, teacher, baseball coach, high school principal, and District Athletic Director.

I learned this Fredrick Douglass quote in high school:

"It is easier to build strong children than to repair broken men." This quote of Douglass has served me well.

First off, when the 1973-74 school year started, about 500 White kids from South Tulsa descended on North Tulsa at the Booker T. Washington High School. Whites came to what had been our school since 1913 with an attitude, exemplifying their right to participate in the activities at Booker T fully.

Perhaps, rightly so. But it would take time for Black students to come to the same conclusion. I am positive that the entire Black student body did not embrace them at the beginning. As a school leader, it was my obligation to do my part to assist in a peaceful transition. These were certainly trying times, as most change is.

The first thing they had to learn; we did not call our school Tulsa Washington High. We were the embodiment of the legendary Booker T. Washington; thus, the student body from times immemorial paid constant homage to Booker T.

This was as it should be.

That junior year of high school was a period of adjustment. While race relations in Tulsa had calmed down considerably since that terrible night on Memorial Day 1921, the start of the school term in 1973 marked one of the few times in fifty-two years that a large contingent of Whites from South Tulsa had crossed over the railroad track into North Tulsa.

Much mistrust had rolled over the dam by this time. Still, there was uncertainty. The times begged the question:

How to relate to people in an integrated setting in a city segregated for its entire history?

Athletics has played an enormous role in our history of bringing people together.

It was the same with the 1973-74 Booker T. Washington football team. That squad went 11-0 and ended the season with a resounding 39-7 state championship over Nathan Hale High School.

Winning helped smooth the transition; having worked in educational settings for a career, I have found winning athletic teams help set an excellent school climate.

Teachers at Booker T. did not teach the history of the Tulsa Race Massacre, nor did any of the public schools in Tulsa; we were aware that seldom did anyone from South Tulsa cross over the railroad track and visit us. In a sense, we did not know the White people who lived in Tulsa, and they did not know us.

Nothing explains the topsy turvy world of my senior high school year like the Booker T. Washington High Yearbook, 1975. To begin with, the front of the book was at the back. The back of the book was at the front of the book.

At least, the editorial board, guided by its editor Connie Cole and the adviser Ms. Barbara Brewer, asked readers to open the book on the back. This methodology was an oddity in one respect.

First, whoever heard of publishing a book backward, it was different, so was our school year. The idea, in retrospect, made a lot of sense.

Following the index that listed each pupil and teacher's name and their picture page, Connie Cole summed up the tumultuous second year of school desegregation in Tulsa, Oklahoma, from the White perspective. With a photograph of two White kids of about the age of first graders playing with balloons, Cole muses:

"Fourteen people came together this year to create a memory. To give you something to look back on. To reminisce and to laugh over. We've been excited, and we've been upset. We attempted the unusual and reached for the unique. The book that opened from the back, the cover without orange and black were just steps to pave the way for BTW's yearbook to become as creative as the mind can be. The '75 Hornet tried to capture all the moments that made it neat being here. The quiet times, the tense and happy times made this book, but more importantly, each of us made this book by being ourselves."

Following her foreword, Coles begins with a quote that hopefully is the place we all ended following this new experience in education and race relations:

"We hope someday words like 'race' will only pertain to cross country or roller derby."

Unfortunately, forty-seven years later, we are still waiting on that day.

While there was resentment with the plan to integrate Booker T., it had less to do with race than the fact that some of my friends were bused out of the community to previously White schools and not allowed to attend Booker T.

I grew up with friends who lived across the street from Booker T. They rode buses to South Tulsa to school. I didn't particularly appreciate separation from my friends; we were coming into the last two years of our high school years. It just didn't seem right.

The school board came up with this plan for selecting one Black Student from North Tulsa to attend Booker T. for every White student from South Tulsa.

If more White kids had requested a transfer more of my friends would have been eligible to attend their neighborhood school. While this plan had flaws, at least the doors of dear Booker T. Washington High School would remain open.

I was hoping that what happened to Carver Jr. High – it was closed – wouldn't happen to Booker T.

In 1971, Carver was closed in what was supposed to be my ninth-grade year at the beloved North Tulsa Junior High.

Following the closing of Carver, I initially attended Freedom School. A school set up by community activists, retired Black administrators, and teachers in a church near the Carver campus.

My grandmother Jeanne B. Goodwin taught one of the courses at Freedom School.

Freedom School offered no athletic programs. Finally, my parents gave in to my request to be bussed to Orville Wright Jr. High School so I could continue playing basketball.

It was a good experience, but I should have stayed at Freedom School. I was unaware that my high school years would provide a reality check in real-world views.

These were changing times in Tulsa and America. Despite the changes, I learned so much during my junior and senior years of high school.

For the second time in my life, I had White classmates, and while I had always played baseball with White kids during the summers in Cherryvale, Kansas, I had White high school baseball teammates for the first time in Tulsa.

Athletics transcends race. Everyone on the team is working for the same goal.

These two experiences would serve me well when I became a high school teacher, baseball coach, assistant principal, and Redan High School Principal in Stone Mountain, Georgia.

"G-O-O-D-Y"

Greg "Goody" Goodwin dressed in his baseball uniform with his dog Toby. In the background is George Washington Carver Jr. High and in the distance is the football stadium where Booker T. Washington High School played their football games at that time. Photo is from the Goodwin collection.

Greg Goodwin is fourth from left on the front row with his high school classmates. Photo from the Booker T. Washington High School Yearbook.

When I began my tenure at Redan High School in 1986, as a social studies teacher and assistant baseball coach, it was a majority White school, with a White principal, and a majority White baseball team.

In 2022, due to White flight into other districts and private schools, Redan is a ninety-nine percent Black school with mostly Black teachers and all Black administrators. The more things change, the more they stay the same.

In 1975, I had no idea that I would spend most of my professional life as an educator and coach. I did not know that I would need skills in dealing with multi-racial people in a group setting to perform teacher, coach, principal and district athletic director tasks.

In the summer of 1973, the Transition Committee selected me as one of the student leaders. Our task was to develop a smooth transition into integration. Dealing with the challenging experiences as junior and senior class president prepared me to handle the professional tasks life presented later.

How did Booker T. prepare me?

This question is an obvious question to ask. The answer, however, may be elusive at best but likely a combination of factors.

It has to do with the rich heritage of Booker T. Washington High School in the life of Blacks in North Tulsa.

From the beginning of its existence, education was a prized possession that every Black family within North Tulsa sought to obtain.

My great grandfather J. H. Goodwin settled his family in Tulsa because of the promise of a better educational system for his children than was provided for them in Water Valley, Mississippi.

Booker T. became the community's crowning jewel.

From the beginning, everybody in North Tulsa pointed to Booker T. with pride, and the people still pump out their chests today when talking about her past, present, and hopefully future.
I say hopefully its future because the current demographics shows Booker T. at an all-time low Black student enrollment (29%).

Perhaps, this was the design all along, fifty-one years in the making.

If you want to understand the resilience of the people of North Tulsa, you must understand what the high school meant to the North Tulsa community.

The community leaders had that frontier spirit. They wanted the absolute best for their community, so when it came time to name their new high school, the community split down the middle on a name that would give hope and direction for the children of Greenwood.

A hot debate ensued over naming the school; for racial accommodationist Booker T. Washington or the radical sociologist William Edward Burghardt DuBois.

Both men were frequent visitors to the frontier and respected for what they brought to the table. Some residents believed that Washington's independent philosophy, do for self, suited the business acumen of the Greenwood community.

While others believed that Black Oklahomans should take a more aggressive stance in advocating for equality under the law rather than acquiescing to inequality, this group urged naming the new high school for Dr. DuBois.

But once the debate settled, most of North Tulsa rallied around the name Booker T. Washington, and the school became the pathway to success for many children raised in Tulsa and neighboring cities.

Because the Tulsa County School Board did not fund education for Blacks, Black schools were built and maintained by a special tax levied on Blacks living in the Greenwood area.

This arrangement ended in 1954 with the *Brown v. Topeka Board of Education* case, which, supposedly, struck down the "separate but equal" standard that had been the law of the land since the 1896 *Plessy v. Ferguson* case. The *Plessy* case legalized segregated facilities in America.

Because Blacks had paid for and maintained Booker T., it gave the school a special place in the hearts of North Tulsa residents.

It was OUR school!

This feeling caused our performing arts and athletic teams to give their best in regional and state competitions. Each ribbon, trophy, and each championship won in competition brought much pride to North Tulsa, and the people who were separated from the rest of the city by a railroad track.

In 1921, Seymour E. Williams was named head football coach at Booker T., the name most often used by alumni, never Tulsa Washington High. Williams served as coach until 1951. He built Booker T. into a powerhouse throughout Oklahoma and beat teams as far away as Chicago, Illinois.

Six years after surviving the fires of the Tulsa Race Massacre, Booker T. became the first Black school in Oklahoma to become fully accredited.

Four years later, Booker T. graduated one of its most noteworthy students, Dr. John Hope Franklin.

In 1948 Ellis Walker Woods, the only principal Booker T. had ever known, died after 35 years of pushing the students at Booker T. to exceed any heights obtained by anyone anywhere on the globe.

Woods had true grit.

In 1913 when he heard that the people of Greenwood were starting a high school, he walked from Memphis to Tulsa to apply for the job. His dogged determination earned him the contract.

Life in Greenwood revolved around Booker T., and the school was the heartbeat of the community. It reaffirmed all that was good about Greenwood.

We were bound by law and fate without knowing the past that had twisted us together and wrapped us in this grand experiment to see if White and Black kids could attend school together in peace and harmony.

Because we knew extraordinarily little about each other's history and social mores, a "Black Students' Only Assembly," which had traditionally been held days before the Christmas holidays at Booker T., caused issues in December 1974. This tradition created tension among the excluded White students.

The yearbook staff memorialized it this way:

*"Two things contributed to diminishing our spirits, though. Our vacation was cut short. The other occurring right before vacation started was the summons to an all-black assembly. The original purpose of this assembly may not have been intended as harmful, but obviously, the results were. It seemed to cause tension and resentment between the races since after vacation, this resentment and tension resulted in strained black-white relations, and graffiti on the bathroom walls, which portrayed both races' opinions on whose school it was."*

Some of our White classmates did not understand that Blacks only assembled because of a tradition dating from 1948 when E. C. Cole replaced Woods as principal of Booker T.

Cole began a series of assemblies each Friday. The boys were required to wear a coat and tie to school, and the girls wore their Sunday dresses.

Mr. Cole invited guest speakers from the community to inspire the students to become the best. There was not a shortage of local success stories. It seemed that almost every adult in Greenwood was a successful business person or a success on the job.

On Fridays, when Mr. Cole did not have a guest speaker, he led discussions on current events. These assembly programs instilled pride in the Booker T. student. The Friday assemblies continued, but the administration eliminated the dress code.

When the 1974-75 school year began, there were many new adjustments for the students, teachers, and administrators.

None of the remaining Black teachers or administrators had a plan to continue the Friday assembly programs.

I am not sure who decided to call a Black-only assembly program just before Christmas break in 1974.

Black administrators intended to give the Black students a chance to reflect on the first half of the school year to return to school in January with their loins girded. Hopefully, in preparation for the successful conclusion of the school year for "underclassmen" and for the seniors to refocus on who they were and what impact they would have on the world as adults.

These types of discussions which Mr. Cole held on Fridays, were taken for granted when we were in a segregated school.

Teachers and administrators believed it was their duty to teach Black kids to be successful and productive citizens.

A good guess is that my seventeen-year-old mind did not see the clarity in this controversy back in 1974, but in retrospect, this would appear to be the well-intended guidance of Booker T.'s adult Black leaders.

They knew what the Booker T. teacher had always given to the Booker T. student.

Those teachers knew to mold us to deal with the changing world of the 1970s, post-assassination of Dr. Martin Luther King, Jr., was their reason for being.

And no amount of interference from the county board of education, which had ignored mainly Black education and Black educators before the impetus to combine public education in Tulsa, was going to stop them from nurturing their Black students.

No one expected the push-back from White students. Their resistance to fall in lockstep behind the Black students at Booker T. caught us off guard.

In our opinion, they were interlopers, gatecrashers, and meddlers in what had been the pride of North Tulsa since the dawn of the 20th century.

"The nerve of them," the Black students collectively thought when word got out that a White girl applied to become Miss Hornet, the name traditionally given to our school queen.

In the 1974-1975 school year, the irony of this educational transformation is: Whites from the south had invaded our school.

Our exclusive terrain, since Oklahoma's admittance into the union, then commenced to claim her as their own.

As if our cultural history up to that point did not exist. In their present, the past and all that had come before them did not matter, or so it seemed. Change is complex, and we were learning to handle change.

Several Black students went about those first couple of years with our guards up, ready to defend the honor of Booker T. and the North Tulsa ethos.

Yet, we lowered our guard just enough to peek out to see if there were places where we could find common ground.

All of us, Black and White, were teenagers trying to understand who we were and how we would fit in the adult world to come.

Much of what I learned at Booker T. had manifested during my work as a professional educator at Redan High School.

Greg Goodwin in the Booker T. Washington High School gym during a ceremony commemorating the placing of a banner in his honor for his athletic contributions to the baseball program during his athletic career at his alma mater. Photo from the Goodwin collection.

Many young people, Black and White, have benefited from the turbulence of my last two years in high school. After all, there are good and bad people of all races. Doing right and treating people right is not bound by race. As with most changes, we adjusted and went on to graduation as the "Mighty 1975 Class at Booker T."

*Part Three*
# Land of the Golden Sunshine

## "G-O-O-D-Y"

*"In the land of golden sunshine, By the Cumberland's fertile shore. Stands a school for greater service, one that we adore. Alma Mater, how we love thee, Love thy WHITE and BLUE! May we strive to meet thy mandates With Faith that's TRUE! Many come to thee for knowledge, Come from East, North, South, and West. For they know that Thou dost offer."*

L. M. Averitte and Clarence Hayden Wilson
Tennessee State University School Song

Tennessee State baseball players who came from the East, North, South, and West to forge a lifetime friendship committed to winning and serving humankind; enjoy a photo at an alumni function. Picture from the Goodwin collection.

My cousin David Goodwin, another Goodwin who is called "Goody" by his close friends, tells a story of a dare that my grandfather issued to me. My grandfather challenged me to jump over a split rail fence, that separated the back yard from the acreage on the farm and if I could do it, he would pay for me to go to Tennessee State University. I completed that feat, he says.

I don't recall this challenge. My grandfather and I were always doing things together. I do remember jumping over the railing. I did it all the time. Maybe I took that bet because I had made that jump so often. Jumping that rail is probably the only time I outsmarted my grandfather.

In any event, without the benefit of a baseball scholarship, I boarded a plane in the fall of 1975. I packed the same trunk my grandfather and his father used previously in their travels. I flew into Nashville to begin my freshman year at Tennessee State University, the land of the golden sunshine, founded in 1912, a year before the business community in Greenwood organized my high school.

Tennessee State was started for similar reasons as my high school; to give Blacks in Middle Tennessee educational opportunities to better their lives. The campus sits near the Cumberland River, and at a particular time of day, the sun's rays descend upon Tennessee State University in a spectacular array of golden hues.

The guiding principles that undergird the Tennessee State University Mission are inscribed above the administration building and other facilities throughout the campus:

"Think, Work, Serve."

Those words were the guiding principles at Booker T. Washington High School.

The expectation: To do a lot of thinking and work hard when we enrolled there, and then, once we finished our studies, to serve humanity throughout the world.

In Tulsa, I had been a big fish in a small pond. My family was well known, and my parents provided a good style of living for their family. Like my siblings, I served in leadership roles in the church and school activities.

I was excited to leave home for college. When the plane approached Nashville, I was still riding the sweet high of excitement. Landing in Nashville at Berry Field, my dad's sister, Jeanne Arradondo, and her husband, Dr. John Arradondo, a Harvard educated physician picked me up at the airport. They lived in Nashville and currently reside there.

My aunt Jeanne, a sociologist, asked if I wanted to go by their house before going to the campus. The adrenaline pumped more excitement to my brain, I was in a hurry to get to the campus and start my college life, so I told them that I wanted to go straight to the campus.

When we arrived on campus at Tennessee State University, it was like a dream come true. As an adolescent, I daydreamed about the places I read about in *JET Magazine*, and those places seemed so far out of my reach. But here I stood on the campus that I had dreamed one day I would attend and wear the white and blue as a baseball team member.

My uncle helped me get my luggage out of the car. My aunt Jeanne and uncle John made sure that I was at the right dorm, got me checked in, instructed me to call them if I needed anything, and they drove off.

Other than the Arradondo family, the only other connection I had to Tennessee State University was an agricultural building on campus named for my great uncle Wilfred Lawson.

He was a contemporary to George Washington Carver and a leading agriculturist in the South at Tennessee Agricultural and Industrial College [Tennessee A & I], now known as Tennessee State University.

He worked at both Tuskegee Institute and Alabama Agricultural and Mechanical College. I had never met him but had been informed of him and his status by my grandmother.

While at Tennessee State University, I did not tell any of my friends or professors that Lawson Hall bore my great uncle's name. I did not want to embarrass the family legacy in case it turned out that I was not a good student. Finally, I felt comfortable enough in my success at Tennessee State that I let some of my friends in on the family history and my connection I had to TSU, prior to my graduation in 1979.

The Arradondos drove off, suddenly, I felt all alone. It was scary and frightening. I was as scared as I had ever been in my life, standing in a strange place and surrounded by people I did not know. I had never been to Nashville.

It was the first time in my life that I had been so far away from home without my usual support system. I had visited a couple of college campuses, but this was the first time I beheld the land of the "golden sunshine," a place that would become my home for the next six years, a place forever in my heart. It also happened to be my second time on an airplane. Perhaps the word I should

## "G-O-O-D-Y"

use was lonely as opposed to afraid. In any event, it was an uncomfortable feeling.

I looked around and saw upper-level students going about their business, laughing, "shooting the breeze," and generally having fun. I didn't know anybody. I caught the elevator to the sixth floor at Watson Hall 1.

When I arrived at my assigned room on the sixth floor, I walked in and met my roommate, Lawrence Nichols from Detroit, and his mom. Seeing them, I relaxed a bit, and it appeared as if Lawrence blew a sigh of relief too. Michael "Marvin Gaye" Fells, a brother from Alexandria, Virginia and I also became friends.

Michael Fells remains one of my closest friends today. During those first few weeks at Tennessee State University, my life centered around my classes and making new friends.

And then, the month of September came, which meant fall baseball practice started. The baseball diamond steadied me. I was around a group of guys who loved baseball as much as I did.

I was in my element and getting to know the guys on the baseball team gave me a set of friends at Tennessee State University that I laughed and had fun with when not hitting the books or going to all the parties.

Such was life at my Historically Black College/University.

I befriended two fellow freshmen, Chris Biles, and Jeffery Martin, who were cousins. They lived in McMinnville, Tennessee, and going home with them became the first of many road trips. I met their younger cousin Reggie Bonner, and we would become lifelong partners.

Campus life, including the student government, did not capture my attention because I was in a new environment and wanted to conquer one domain at a time, so I stayed focused on my studies and making the baseball team when practice started. Looking back I should have involved myself in student government, as I did in high school.

I received baseball scholarship offers from Langston University and John Brown College, but my heart desired Tennessee State University. When Coach Jacob Robinson wrote back and told me that I could try out for the team, my mind stayed on Tennessee State. I was going to Tennessee State University come rain, snow, or sunshine. And I was going to make Coach Robinson's team.

Frankly, I knew I could play baseball. The first base position was a position I had played sparingly in high school, but Tennessee State University had a senior pitcher named Nathaniel Snell, who played first base when he did not pitch.

Snell signed a professional baseball contract at the end of my freshman season with the Baltimore Orioles. Snell would eventually pitch in the big leagues with the Orioles. After Snell was drafted, I began my tenure as Tennessee State University's first baseman for the next three years.

Sizing up the team's needs, during my freshman year, I decided to try out for second base, a position I had played in high school with success. I took stock of the level of play on the team, and I knew I could play with the best of them. I made the team.

My freshman year, I started most games at second base, and when Snell pitched I would start at first base where I would start the remainder of my career at Tennessee State after Snell's departure to the professional ranks.

During the early days of fall practice, I bonded with another freshman named Kenneth Cheyenne Joyce; everyone called him "Chey." He was born and raised in Nashville, not far from Tennessee State University. He took me home with him and introduced me to his parents, Ernest Joyce, Sr., and Fannie Mae Joyce.

The Joyce family treated me like a member of their family. Although I had an uncle and aunt in Nashville, it was good to have the Joyce family so close by the school.

Shortly before I met the Joyce family, tragedy struck their household. Kenneth had two brothers who were twins, named Ronnie and Donnie Joyce.

Ronnie and Donnie were the double-play combination at TSU in 1974. Ronnie played second base, and Donnie played shortstop. By all accounts, the Joyce boys were superb baseball players.

Before I arrived in Nashville - the summer of 1974 - Ronnie was hanging around an abandoned house in an alley near the Joyce home. The Nashville police raided the house. The police shot and killed Ronnie as he fled the abandoned house.

So, this 21st-century phenomenon of young, unarmed Black men being gunned down by police officers is nothing new. There is no way in the world an unarmed young man should end up dead for participating in a victimless crime like hanging out with neighborhood friends in an abandoned house for a few minutes. Unfortunately, young Black men were taught to run from the police in those days.

Today, we teach our kids to comply with commands of police officers and to remain as calm as possible.

Like today's Black Lives Matter protests, the city of Nashville was up in arms over the senseless killing of Ronnie Joyce.

He had a promising career in baseball; obtaining a degree from Tennessee State University would have guaranteed his future success.

All Ronnie could have been, and the contributions he would have made to humanity, destroyed by Nashville's over-policing of the Black community.

Learning the story of Ronnie Joyce had a profound impact on me. It made me further realize the enormous opportunity that each of us has and must use to be of service.

In a way, my commitment to community service derives from knowing that a young person gets cut down in a split second if not careful. This belief is not a knock on the good police officers that protect and serve.

Befriending "Chey" was like gaining a whole other family. He was a local high school legend. His sweet but tough-as-nails mom, Mrs. Fannie Mae Joyce, told me that I did not have to wait on Chey to bring me to the house.

She said I could come over whenever I wanted. I jumped on that opportunity. I would walk to Joyce's house, cutting through Hadley Park, and eat there often. The back door usually stayed unlocked.

"Chey" was the only Freshman on a full baseball scholarship. He and I made the starting lineup as freshmen. I played second base when Snell pitched and first base when he was on the mound.

I still tease "Chey" today about who got the first hit in our first collegiate baseball game against Alabama State. Of course, it was me, or I couldn't tease him. Chey's brother "Twin" [Donnie] was a senior on the 1976 Tennessee State University ball club, and he appointed me as his rookie for that season. I gained two brothers.

"Chey" played third base and catcher. He was one of the best baseball players I ever played with or against in my career.

Oliver Cooper, an outfielder from Highland Park, Michigan, and Chris Biles, a catcher from McMinnville, Tennessee, were other freshmen who contributed to our inaugural 1976 collegiate season.

I went out for the baseball team with the attitude that I wanted to make the baseball program as well known nationally as the football, basketball, and track teams.

The baseball team was started at TSU in the early 1950s by Samuel Whitmon. As a student, he played football at Tennessee State University and was an All-American running back. He later served as an assistant football coach, and the first head baseball coach at TSU.

By the time I arrived on campus in 1975, Whitmon was the Athletic Director, and the once-proud baseball program had become average at best. My mission was to revive baseball at TSU. I wanted Tennessee State University baseball to be as revered nationally as the football team, and the band were in HBCU lore.

Coach Jacob Robinson, an outstanding baseball player at David Lipscomb College, was head baseball coach my freshman year. He left to become the head baseball coach at Kentucky State University after my freshman year.

Coach Allen Robinson became the Head Baseball Coach my sophomore year. Coach Allen Robinson had been a big-time two-sport athlete (football and baseball) at Tennessee State.

Allen Robinson signed a professional contract with the Chicago Cubs after his college career. He was signed to this contract by the legendary "Buck" O'Neil, who scouted for the Chicago Cubs. O'Neil later became the first Black coach in Major League Baseball.

O'Neil received induction into the Major League Baseball Hall of Fame in 2022.

O'Neil had a fascinating career in the Negro Leagues; he played alongside Satchel Paige and made several memorable moments during his time with the Kansas City Monarchs. He served as the guest speaker for the baseball banquet at the end of my sophomore season at Tennessee State.

In 1977, Larry Cole, who was a teammate of Robinson at TSU, assisted Coach Robinson. He served as the infielders' coach. Coach Cole was a stickler for leadership. Early in the 1977 pre-season drills, Coach Cole announced that he was looking for a captain. I stepped up and told Coach Cole that I was his man. Coach Cole said he wasn't sure if I would be on the baseball team.

Undaunted and amused, I proceeded to demonstrate my leadership ability to Coach Cole and my teammates. No player or coach outworked or outhustled me on the field. I left everything on the practice field. It did not take Coach Cole long to name me the team captain.

I led by example in this leadership role and always talked to my teammates, encouraging them to rise to the occasion. My teammate and lifelong friend, Curtis Burke, called me the voice of the Tigers because I was boisterous on the field.

Burke played the outfield and could hear me yelling encouragement to the team from my first base position. I was well established in my junior year when the hard-hitting Burke joined our squad from Columbia, South Carolina.

One day during Burke's freshman year, I invited him to my apartment.

I showed him a twelve-inch picture. The picture hanging on the wall proclaimed, "I AM THE GREATEST."

Burke asked me why I brought him to my apartment and showed him that picture.

I told him that he could not play for us if he did not think he, too, was the greatest.

I always sought ways to inspire myself and those around me to succeed. Baseball is a team game, and success comes from several individuals performing successfully.

Left to Right Nathaniel Snell and Greg "Goody" Goodwin in Atlanta to play a game against Morris Brown College, 1976. Photo from the Goodwin collection.

Burke went on to have a great freshman year and baseball career at Tennessee State University and concluded his playing days with several years in the minor leagues after being selected with the third-round pick by the Houston Astros in 1981.

I knew that if I was going to talk, as they say, the talk, I had to walk the walk. When the game was on the line, a teammate or I would come up with a clutch hit or catch to save the day for Tennessee State University. I can proudly state that during my four seasons (1976-1979) at Tennessee State University, we never experienced a losing season.

At the end of my senior year, I was in the top ten in stolen bases in the nation and ended my career with nearly a .350 batting average. I saved many ball games with nifty footwork around the bag at first. I was fortunate to play with so many talented teammates. If they are keeping score, it does matter if you win.

In 1979, my senior year, we had the best record in the history of baseball at Tennessee State University; we finished that year 30-12. Franchises in Major League Baseball drafted seven guys from the 1979 team.

A freshman phenom, Terry Blocker, later played in the big leagues after being drafted by the New York Mets in the first round in 1981.

Also, the Montreal Expos drafted Kirk "Frisco" Forbes in the 11th round. He played second base, and very few ground balls got through the right side of the infield.

My senior year I stole 41 bases in 42 attempts, which ranked me nationally in the top ten among base stealers in 1975, from the archives.

We lived with an upperclassman, John "True Blue" Thomas, in the first apartment I lived in off-campus.

That experiment didn't last long as our landlord made us split up after one semester.

There was too much noise and traffic coming in and out of the apartment. Also, Dennis "Dean" Seats, a sure-handed shortstop from Chicago, and Blocker and Forbes were significant contributors to that 1979 squad.

There have been eight Tennessee State University student-athletes who have played major league baseball. I played with three of them and coached another one.

Those big league players I either played with or coached are Roy Johnson (1978-1980), Nate Snell (1973-78), Terry Blocker (1978-81), and Everett Stull (1990-91). I coached Stull at Redan High School.

During my freshman year Kindell Stephens, the Sports Information Director, took an interest in me. Stephens knew that I came from a newspaper background, so he offered me a job helping him out in the sports information office.

Each year Stephens gave me more and more responsibilities. Eventually, he listed me as the Assistant Sports Information Director while I was still in undergraduate school. I only returned home during Christmas breaks after my first year in college.

By my senior year, I had keys to all the athletic buildings on campus. If there were two athletic events on campus, Stephens would supervise one, sending me to handle the other one.

The Tennessee State University Athletic Department staff. Photo from TSU Yearbook

Like me, Stephens had been a college athlete.

He played basketball at Fisk University and spent a brief stint in the National Basketball Association with the Los Angeles Lakers.

Stephens was close friends with Ted "The Hound" McClain. "The Hound" starred in basketball at Tennessee State University, then had a significant career in the American Basketball Association. He also played in the National Basketball Association.

"Hound" knew Ervin "Magic" Johnson and brought "Magic" to campus to help raise money for the basketball program. I got to meet "Magic" during his rookie season with the Lakers during "Hound's" NBA fundraiser game at Tennessee State in the summer of 1977.

Since Stephens knew firsthand the perils of a young man putting all his eggs in the basket of a professional athletic career, he always cautioned me that getting an education was why I was in school.

Stephens mentored me until the day he died in January 2008. He taught me how to handle adversity. More importantly, he taught me that trouble was always waiting around the corner.

What will you do when you turn the corner and adversities are staring you in the face. Kindell was a tremendous role model and great big brother to me.

At the end of the workday, Stephens would meet with Ted "The Hound" McClain and Frank Pillow, Sr., his tight buddies, and go to the YMCA to play basketball.

From L-R Greg "Goody" Goodwin, Curt "Frisco" Forbes, Robert Rowland, and Curtis "Big Poison" Burke, Tennessee State baseball alumni brothers, teammates for life. This Photo is from the Goodwin collection.

Both McClain and Pillow grew up in Nashville. They attended the legendary Pearl High School and earned scholarships to Tennessee State University in basketball and football respectively.

This group of young Black men would take me along with them, and we would play basketball. Hanging out with these three men not only kept me out of trouble - never having much idle time - but I learned so much about personal character, problem-solving, and what it meant to be a mature adult.

I had an abundance of guidance growing up in Tulsa but having a village in Nashville was priceless.

These three men were interested in my growth and development. They freely gave their insight on a sundry of subjects, and I took in all the lessons they taught me by precepts and examples. I have told them thanks many times for being so supportive of me as a college student-athlete.

I majored in political science. By the time I graduated, the university had changed the name of the major to Government and Public Affairs.

Also, I graduated with enough hours to earn a minor in education which required me to complete a student teaching program.

I am not sure why I took so many education courses. I honestly had no desire to teach; I didn't think. I'm happy I took those education courses now.

While I had many family members who were school teachers, teaching school never actually crossed my mind. I did not think I could earn sufficient money to raise a family, so when I graduated, a career in education was the furthest profession from my mind.

Besides that, I had always dreamed of playing professional baseball for a living. It is the one thing that I wanted to do above all else growing up in Tulsa.

Seven of my baseball team members were drafted or signed free-agent contracts with a major league franchise in my senior year at Tennessee State University.

Since I did not get drafted or sign a free agent contract, I went to Los Angeles and conversed with officials from the San Francisco Giants. I knew Jose Cardenal, a former major leaguer who married a young woman from Tulsa.

The Cardenals daughter, Bridget, and I were friends and maintain a friendship until this day. She alerted her dad that I was interested in continuing my baseball career. He served as a consultant for the San Francisco Giants at that time.

Cardenal was instrumental in arranging the free-agent tryout. I went to California for two weeks working out with the Giants but did not receive a baseball contract. Sooner or later, every athlete must realize that their athletic career is over. Luckily, you can always be a professional in another profession.

When I did not receive a baseball contract, it looked like the end of the road for my involvement in baseball.

## "G-O-O-D-Y"

It was hard for me to imagine life without baseball. I had given so much passion and energy to the game.

I went back to Nashville and enrolled in a master's program in public administration at TSU. Kindell Stephens welcomed me back to campus, and I continued working as his assistant.

The best thing for me, was being awarded a graduate assistantship through the Sports Information Department. I was back at my second home for the next two years, in the "Land of the Golden Sunshine."

During homecoming of the 1979-80 academic year, I ran into Cynthia Counts. Cynthia and I had attended undergraduate school together.

Cynthia caught my eye the moment I saw her on campus in 1975. I was interested in her but could never strike up a meaningful conversation with her. She was an exceptional student.

While in high school at Southeast High School in Kansas City, Missouri, she dreamed of going to the University of Southern California after graduation.

However, luckily for me, Cynthia did not want to place the financial strain of attending the University of Southern California on her parents; she never applied.

Like myself, she gained admission to Tennessee State University, so she enrolled in the school where the golden rays shined in a spectacular array on most days.

My mama always said that first impressions could be lasting impressions. Cynthia and I started dating towards the end of our freshman year.

At this time, I appeared locked in, concentrating on mastering the books and staying academically eligible for collegiate baseball. Just the kind of guy, an intelligent girl, enjoyed being around.

Cynthia went back home to Kansas City during the summer break, and we continued to talk over the telephone when we could. There were no cell phones back then. Long-distance telephone fare was astronomical.

At the end of the summer, we reconnected on campus. Returning to campus after the summer, I was a sophomore coming off a big year as a Tennessee State University baseball team member.

I felt my oats as a big man on campus; after all, I now knew how the upperclassmen felt the year before when I arrived on campus terrified of my new experience.

I knew my way around campus, and I was having a good time, hanging out with my buddies, and doing the fun things college guys do. I was a happy-go-lucky sophomore living my dream of playing baseball at Tennessee State University.

At the beginning of our second year in college, Cynthia saw me as a carefree jock and one who did not take life too seriously. I did not seem to fit into her serious-mindedness. She was brilliant and exceedingly beautiful.

Suddenly, we were not talking as often as we had over the summer. We drifted apart. Yet the lines of communication remained open.

I kept talking to her throughout our undergraduate days, and then we graduated. Cynthia returned home to Kansas City and accepted a position with the Federal Reserve Bank of Kansas City in 1979.

Just before graduation that spring, Cynthia had a car accident around the corner from the apartment where she stayed. She had left the car in Nashville, but that fall, she came back during homecoming week to pick up her car.

Cynthia Counts Goodwin, Greg "Goody" Goodwin, and State Representative Regina Goodwin, District 73, Tulsa, Oklahoma. Photo from the Goodwin collection.

As fate would have it, I enrolled in a master's program in Public Administration at TSU. I was not going to waste another opportunity to win her heart.

After the homecoming game, we struck up a long-distance relationship.

Perhaps, Cynthia saw that despite the appearance of being a happy-go-lucky guy, that sophomore from Tulsa had graduated on time and returned to school to pursue a master's degree in public administration. Maybe there was hope for me after all.

While in graduate school I spent a lot of time with Larry Wilhoite, whom I had befriended in undergrad. He had been an outstanding athlete in the Nashville area, and we had some great times playing in a softball league during that period.

We are close partners today. We have a saying we still use: "No Use Years."

It took two years to finish up the masters. When I graduated, my aunt Susan Goodwin Jordan lived in Houston, Texas. She got me a position with the Dowell Oil Company. So around September 1981, I moved to Victoria, Texas.

Dowell put me through a training program to become a field production manager. The position required me to work in the oil fields every day. It was hot and greasy in those oil fields. I worked at Dowell for about one and one-half years. It was hard work.

I quickly discovered I didn't particularly appreciate working in the oil field. The money was excellent, though.

During my employment there was one requirement. I had to obtain a commercial driver's license.

While at Dowell, I met David Green who became my roommate in Victoria, Texas. He became the godfather of Lindsay, my second born.

David graduated from the other TSU, as in Texas Southern University. He eventually left Dowell and went on to have a successful 30-year career with the Internal Revenue Service. He was a standup guy, and I am grateful for my time at Dowell because of meeting Dave.

While at Dowell, I applied for admission to O. W. Coburn Law School at Oral Roberts University. The law school opened its doors in 1979. In 1983, I moved back to Tulsa and traded the smell of oil for the scent of law books.

About four Black students enrolled in the law school with me, making us some of its first students and, most certainly, among its first Black students.

The law school bore Orin Wesley Coburn's name, a donor to the law school and founder of Coburn Optical Industries.

His son Tom Coburn would later become a United States Senator. Although I do not recall meeting her, Michele Bachman, a future senator from Minnesota and a 2016 candidate for the Republican nomination for President of the United States, was enrolled in the school at the time.

Law school seemed logical for me after the major leagues did not come calling, and I did not like the toils of an oil field production manager. My dad had spent some time in law school. His father was a lawyer, and I had an uncle, Jim, who was a lawyer.

After one semester in law school, I realized that practicing law was not what I wanted to do. I quit after the first semester.

Law school is the only thing that I have ever walked away from in life. I cannot explain why other than to say I did not feel the passion for a career as a lawyer.

Simply put, upholding the legal system did not seem like my purpose in life. I did not know what I would do in life, but I knew being a lawyer was not it. I continued my search to find my way.

When I was withdrawing from law school, my girlfriend, Cynthia Counts, was transferred to the Federal Reserve Bank in Denver, Colorado.

I followed her to Denver. I had several relatives in Denver. All my mom's sisters and brothers were in Denver. Also, I had a cousin, Michelle, who grew up to become Ms. Black Colorado. Her husband, Clark Beauchamp, was an entrepreneur.

In the early days of cable television, Beauchamp opened Innovative Technical Systems (ITS). He sold cable television equipment. I went to work for ITS in their warehouse, learning the business.

I quickly received a promotion. I sold television cable equipment for the firm. I felt like I had found my niche in life.

I became the company's top sales representative. I am a people person, so this position was a natural fit for my personality.

During this period, Cynthia Counts became Mrs. Cynthia Counts Goodwin.

Life was good.

Then Beauchamp had a grand idea to expand his operations to the Atlanta market - the cable television industry was booming. As the company's top sales associate, Beauchamp selected me to open the new Atlanta office.

I talked it over with Cynthia. She investigated the possibility of transferring to the Atlanta Federal Reserve Bank. The Federal Reserve accepted Cynthia's transfer request, and we moved to Atlanta.

The move ended up being great for us as Cynthia would retire from the Federal Reserve Bank as one of their top executives years later.

She probably would have fared just as well had we stayed in Denver. My career, on the other hand, really benefited from the move to Atlanta.

*Part Four*
**Gate City**

## "G-O-O-D-Y"

*Atlanta is known as Gate City. It is the gateway to the South. For me, Atlanta has been the gateway that opened a new vista for expressing my purpose in life.*

**Gregory "Goody" Goodwin**

Shortly after moving to Atlanta, our company went out of business. It was not big enough to compete with the giants in the cable industry. Beauchamp ceased operations in Atlanta.

Now, I was out of a job, and my wife had just transferred to a new location in the federal reserve system. We could not pack up and move back to Denver or a new city. Besides, I did not know if I wanted to continue working in the cable industry.

I had not figured out what I wanted to do next, so I applied for temporary work as a substitute teacher in the Dekalb County School District. I had never wanted to be a teacher. I did not think that teachers made enough money to live a prosperous life. But for some reason, I took enough courses at TSU to earn a minor in education.

I was fortunate to do my student teaching at historic Pearl High School in Nashville. I even had the opportunity to "student teach" for a larger-than-life iconic teacher and coach, Mr. Cornelius Ridley.

Ridley was induction into the Tennessee Secondary Schools Athletic Association (TSSAA) Hall of Fame in 1991.

## "G-O-O-D-Y"

That earlier decision to minor in education turned out to be one of the best decisions made in my young life.

The principal at Miller Grove Middle School in Dekalb County, Georgia, looked favorably on my application. I was all set to work for a couple of weeks, allowing me to bring in a little income and give me a chance to sort out my next career move.

Being a "people person," soon I was all over the school interacting with the students. I was having a ball teaching my classes and talking with the students in the hallway, at lunch, and after school.

When I was playing baseball as a kid, the adults in my life always told me to put my best foot forward on each play because you never knew when a scout would be in the stands evaluating you.

After two weeks of substitute teaching, the principal, Barbara McKee, said she had observed me working with the students all over the school. She felt that my presence was inspirational to them. She asked me, "How would you like to be a permanent substitute teacher."

I laughed and asked how one becomes a permanent substitute teacher. She just laughed and said, "Show up every day, and we will find something for you to do."

I showed up every day. After two months as a permanent substitute teacher, Ms. McKee asked me if I wanted to be a full-time teacher. I accepted the opportunity. When she hired me full-time, Miller Grove was a junior high school with grades from seventh through ninth. Also on the faculty at Miller Grove was Tom Clark. Little did I know then, but Coach Tom would become very instrumental in my career growth.

Since Miller Grove was a feeder school for Redan High School, Coach Clark served as the head varsity baseball coach. Coach Clark hired me as an assistant baseball coach. All it took was a few conversations about my baseball background. I was back in baseball as an assistant varsity baseball coach in 1986.

In 1991, Miller Grove changed from a junior high school to a middle school. The middle school structure only included the seventh and eighth grades. The ninth grade became a part of Redan High School, and since I was a ninth-grade teacher, I moved over to Redan High School.

The baseball program at Redan started in 1977. Gale Coleman led the squad. In his only year at the helm, Coleman finished with a career 6-2 record.

From 1978 through 1983, Jerry Hogan served as head baseball coach at Redan. Hogan compiled a 111-59 record.

In 1985, Coach Clark took over a successful Redan baseball program that sported a .657 winning percentage. From 1985 through 1988, Clark won 91 baseball games, losing only 26 for a winning percentage of .778.

Coach Clark was a remarkably successful baseball coach. In 1988, he accepted a position to coach baseball at Gordon Junior College. He recommended I succeed him at Redan.

At the time, Redan High School was 90 percent white. Coach Clark convinced the principal, Dr. Doyle Oran, that hiring me as the first Black head coach to coach a predominately White baseball team was an excellent workable idea. He was convincing, and I received the job offer.

In four years, Clark had developed an excellent baseball program. My task was to keep it going. I wanted the Redan baseball program to keep striving and keep getting better. I quickly found out that I could not develop a better baseball culture at Redan without impacting the lives of the student-athletes in the program.

Suddenly, my life took a sharp and unpredictable turn without any effort on my part. As a coach, I am back in baseball, the game I love, and teaching school, something I never thought I would do.

I was pleased to get the head coaching position, and I reminded myself that less than ten percent of my salary resulted from my baseball coaching ability. My interest had to be in teaching, where I received the bulk of my salary. I always made sure that I was a teacher first, then a coach. The two would and could not coexist.

The best way to impact their lives was to create a program that ensured every kid who wanted to attend college on a baseball scholarship and had baseball skills to play collegiate baseball had the opportunity to realize their dream.

I developed a Rolodex of college baseball coaches and professional scouts. I constantly called them lobbying for scholarships for my student-athletes. Redan continued sending kids to college baseball programs throughout the country. Also, to several major league franchises.

There were times when I would be out getting gas for my car, and a young man from another school in the county would approach me and ask if I could help them get into college. I would take down their information and make a few calls on their behalf. It did not matter to me what high school they attended.

If I could help a youngster get an education, I did everything in my power to do it. Growing up in Tulsa, my family taught me that "service, i. e., helping others was the rent you pay for room and board on the earth." That was a family motto.

Before I knew it, I was impacting the kids' lives around me, and it made me feel good. I had stumbled into my purpose in life. Maybe my purpose in life had overtaken me and pulled me along a course of doing good in the lives of people in my sphere. I was working with a young man who shared a similar passion for baseball. His name was Edward Dion Williams, he would go on to a hall of fame baseball coaching career at McNair High School. Williams was inducted into the Georgia Dugout Club Hall of Fame in 2021.

We played against each other numerous times and he made me a better coach. We remain the best of friends to this day.

Going to Redan High School every day and teaching school did not seem like work. Coaching elite baseball players or developing average baseball players did not seem like work.

I was having too much fun developing the lives of young people, tugging at them to put their best foot forward, dream the impossible dream, and put the sweat equity into whatever they wanted to do in life. It was gratifying to be a dream maker.

In college, I did not know why I gravitated to so many education courses. Teaching school was not on my radar. I never gave the teaching profession a second thought.

I did not place much value in the fact I had earned a minor degree in education at Tennessee State University and had completed the student teaching requirement under the tutelage of the legendary Cornelius Ridley.

I was also wrong about not being able to provide for a family on a teacher's salary. I wouldn't get rich, but I am comfortable.

But all along, my better angels were preparing me for my life's work. When the time was right, I took to teaching, coaching, and educational administration as effortlessly as birds fly in the sky, as majestic as a dolphin swimming in the ocean, and as effortlessly as I had scooped up an errant throw at first base.

## "G-O-O-D-Y"

While I realized the importance of transforming teenagers into sound young adults, I had to continue the winning ways of Redan baseball on the field.

I coached for twelve years, scoring 228 wins, only losing 96 games, a .704 winning percentage. At the start of the 2021 baseball season, I ranked twelfth for most wins by a Dekalb County head baseball coach and second on the most wins list at Redan behind Marvin Pruitt's 291 wins. I only coached for twelve seasons. I was blessed to coach young men and women who bought into my vision and ethic of hard work.

In the regional playoffs, we played six eventual state champions during my coaching tenure. Redan has won more state playoff games than any school in Dekalb County history, with a state playoff record of 59-52.

I did not win a state championship, going 3-4 in the playoffs, but the old saying during my twelve years as head coach was: *"The road to the state championship goes through Redan."*

In 1990, I had my first player drafted by a major league franchise when the St. Louis Cardinals selected pitcher Ricky Kimball. He accepted a scholarship at Florida State University and was redrafted the following year by the Oakland Athletics.

In 1987, the year Kimball graduated from Redan, I was the assistant baseball coach under the leadership of Coach Clark and played a small part in Kimball's progression to Florida State and professional baseball.

The Expos in 1992 picked Everett Stull out of Tennessee State University by way of Redan High. That same year Pax Briley, who had earned a baseball scholarship to Clemson, was selected by the California Angeles.

Two of my kids were selected straight out of Redan High School in 1993, Corey Lima by the Chicago Cubs, and the Texas Rangers selected Jamil Phillips.

Andy Taulbee was selected in the second round by the San Francisco Giants in 1994 after playing at Clemson. The Toronto Blue Jays picked up Clearance Whatley in 1996 after his senior season at Redan.

After completing college at North Carolina A&T University, Corey Lima was redrafted in 1997 by the Florida Marlins.

In 1999 Redan again had two players sign professional baseball contracts. Jeff Nebel, who graduated from Mercer University that year, signed with the California Angels, and Brandon Phillips was a second-round pick by the Montreal Expos.

"G-O-O-D-Y"

Greg "Goody" Goodwin and Brandon Phillips before a game with the St. Louis Cardinals.

Brandon Phillips went on to have a 17 - year Major League Baseball career. His family is undoubtedly the most incredible athletic family to hail from the Great Redan High School.

Lue and James Phillips raised four children in the Stone Mountain, Georgia area. Their oldest son, Jamil, played professional baseball after his collegiate career at Southern University.

Brandon opted against the scholarship offer from the University of Georgia to sign professionally with the Montreal Expos.

The California Angels selected the Phillips' son, P. J. Phillips, as the third pick in the second round. Rather than accept a collegiate scholarship offer, he elected to sign a professional baseball contract.

Porsha, their youngest child, and daughter played professional basketball after a fantastic career at the University of Georgia (UGA). The parents were terrific supporters of their children. Their philanthropic endeavors have benefitted the entire Redan community and athletic programs.

I listed some of the draft choices that I had the pleasure of coaching; however, it was the relationships I developed with all my players that I enjoyed most.

Whether they signed a professional contract, a scholarship at a Power 5 school, Junior College, or didn't contribute much to our high school squads, I always preached about the value everyone brought to their perspective teams. Every young man or woman that I taught or coached provided value.

I couldn't save every student that I encountered, but I treated every student with respect and demanded discipline and hard work from them all.

I realized that not every student-athlete would get an opportunity to play at the next level. I wanted them to understand playing baseball, softball, basketball, or serving as a student manager at Redan High was the next level.

We had a lot of fun, and we won a lot of games. I never learned to like losing, and my motto while coaching several sports was "Playing To Win." Today, my email handle is "play to win."

At last count, I had assisted more than 500 young women and men in obtaining scholarship opportunities, but who is counting, right. Most of the coaches who coached or guided me during my playing days informed me often that the only way I could pay them back was by assisting others.

My thank you goes out to the following coaches: Charles Sims, Julius Pegues, Rash Brothers (Cherryvale), Emmett Shannon, Wiley Brothers, Ike Taylor, Roy Foster, Irwin Brown, Stan Irvine, Jacob Robinson, Allen Robinson, and Larry Cole (I know I left out a few).

Your guidance was tremendous, and I hope I made you proud.

The following season, 1999, turned out to be my last year as a high school baseball coach. The Atlanta Braves selected Ahmad woods in the ninth round.

I enjoyed the 228 wins in baseball and the 90 wins in girls' softball. A total of 318 wins in the record book, but the most fantastic feeling in the world is to get a kid into college on a "free ride," as we say, and have them come back years later and say, "thank you, Coach."

That's what this journey is all about.

Everett Stull was a talented athlete at Redan. He tried out for the pitcher's position. Although he had a strong arm, he did not have control over his pitches, and during his tenure at Redan, the team had several talented pitchers.

There were just not enough innings for him on the mound at Redan at that time. Also, I was not a very good pitching coach.

I played him every game at third base. At the end of his senior year, I told him that I could get him in school at Tennessee State University as a pitcher if he wanted to give it a try. Stull trusted me.

After three years at Tennessee State University, as a third round draft pick, he signed a professional baseball contract in 1992. We remain great friends to this day.

By 1997 Stull made his way to the major leagues playing for the Montreal Expos, the Atlanta Braves, and the Milwaukee Brewers. Stull appeared in 20 major league games for various clubs. He won two of the five games where he was the pitcher of record.

The moral of this story is: Here is a guy who pitched three innings his senior year of high school and still made it to the big leagues. It's not where you start but where you finish.

Several young men, I have coached wanted to play baseball professionally. The Redan baseball program attempted to provide a pathway to professional baseball.

However, as coaches, we were mindful and realistic that there are not enough professional roster spots for every young man in America, let alone Dekalb County, Georgia, who wants to play in the major leagues.

After all, I, too, dreamed that dream.

At Redan, I focused on education. I imparted to my student-athletes the lessons I learned at TSU from Kindell Stephens, and those were, school is all about preparing one to make a living as a professional in some capacity, as well as serving the needs of your community.

In twelve years coaching baseball at Redan, several players received scholarships to further their education while chasing their dream of playing professional baseball.

I'm proud to say I have not heard of one of my players not contributing to society. The goal remains to turn professional, and it doesn't have to be in athletics.

To sell my guys the idea of striving for an athletic scholarship, I impressed them with the need to set a high standard in the classroom. The books came before baseball. My guys understood that they must first hit the books before they could hit the baseball.

I knew a jock could have good grades and be competitive on the field simultaneously because I did it at Booker T. Washington High School and Tennessee State University.

In my early years at Tennessee State University, I struggled a bit because of distorted priorities, but then I prayed.

There is a joke I often share with my friends:

I told God that if he pulled me through my academic struggles, my firstborn would go to Tennessee State University, but my next child would go to Florida A & M University, our fierce rival in the '70s.

What is not so amusing is that my youngest daughter, Lindsay attended and earned a degree from FAMU.

Very few people talk about my Girls Fastpitch Softball coaching career. I started coaching girls' softball at Redan in 1993 and retired in 1999. I had to learn the game and soon learned that fast pitch softball was very similar to baseball.

I was thrilled when I learned that a softball coach would be competitive if the coach had a pretty good battery. The battery is a baseball term for pitcher and catcher combo.

That year was my first time coaching girls, but athletes are athletes. My final softball coaching record was 90 wins and 44 losses, .672 winning percentage. My combined winning percentage in baseball and softball is .688.

We had some great teams with several amazing athletes. One of my favorite players - coaches, have favorites - was a catcher named Jodi Greenlee. Jodi also babysat the Goodwin kids, like many of my former students. Jodi had this to say about her old ball coach:

*"To say that Coach Goodwin has been vital in my life journey is an understatement. There are few if any, people I continue talking to from high school, but Coach Goodwin has been by my side these past 25 years.*

*In my sophomore year, I first met Coach Goodwin when the Dekalb County School District took on fastpitch softball as an official high school sport. I played travel softball for quite some time and was delighted to have an avenue at the school to play what I loved and excelled at playing. Not all were as enthused, but Coach Goodwin led the team in a manner that I wanted to be a part of the team. We weren't his beloved baseball, but he did what he does best, lead, and I was eager to follow.*

*For me, high school was a time of emotional turmoil. There was a strain on my relationship with my parents, but Coach Goodwin kept me afloat. He believed in me when I didn't believe in myself and when I didn't think anyone could. That was life-changing, and I didn't want to disappoint him. He became like a father to me.*

*Since those days, I have lost my father and have never married. However, when and if that time comes, I expect Coach Goodwin to walk me down the aisle. He has known me longer than most and has loved me through it all. He has seen the good and bad and shown me grace, discipline, love, and excellence. Last year, 2020, I had the privilege of seeing where he grew up, hearing stories from his sister Regina, and visiting monuments erected about his family.*

*I was not surprised at the excellence, bravery, and beauty of his family and his beginnings. His family has made a difference all along the way, and Coach Goodwin is no different. His legacy is enormous, and the ripple effect of his purpose and impact is far-reaching.*

*Today I am a teacher. I love to encourage young people in their worth and help them see that they are stronger than they think and better than they believe. I love to greet them each day and help them see the beauty of the day and the grace of their existence. I genuinely think I can do that, mainly because I had someone do that for me. His name is Coach Goodwin."*

You never know whose life you might be touching. Perhaps I did find my calling.

The guys bought into my plan, and I got busy on the telephone. I made sure college baseball coaches knew

Redan could provide them academically sound student-athletes.

One of the coaches I admired was Roger Cador. He coached baseball for 32 years at Southern University, where he had been a star outfielder in the early 1970s before embarking on his professional career.

Coach Cador and I were very similar; he was interested in his players beyond their performance on the baseball field. He was interested in helping to develop them into productive men in society.

He was also addicted to winning. I did not just send my kids anywhere. The coaches had to offer my kids something more than just baseball. Coach Cador was one of those coaches. So from time to time, I would call him and say, "Coach, I have a young man that I think can help your program, and I know you can help them."

I arranged for Coach Cador to come to Atlanta to sign one of my students. He arrived in town the day before the scheduled signing.

Coach Cador received a call from his wife. She experienced a medical emergency and was taken immediately to the hospital.

## "G-O-O-D-Y"

Soon Cador was on the phone trying to schedule a flight back to Baton Rouge, Louisiana, to be with his wife. He called me to say that he would be flying out early the following day before the scheduled meeting with the athlete and his family.

I cannot recall the student's name, but he received offers from several schools, and Coach Cador was afraid that the young man would sign with another school if he did not sign him that day.

I picked up the phone and arranged a meeting with Cador and the family for 7:00 a. m. the following day. There were smiles all around that morning.

The young man was happy to receive a scholarship to play baseball for an iconic HBCU coach, and Cador was delighted that he could secure the young man's signature in time for him to board his flight back home to attend to his wife.

Coach Cador thanked me, but I did not think I had done anything grand. I did what I do, putting people together, and making them smile. Nothing makes me happier than to see other people enjoying their success.

If I knew a student-athlete at another high school in the Atlanta area who could benefit from the mentorship of Coach Cador, I would call him up and tell him about that young man. I did not just help my players; I helped young people at other high schools in the area get into college. It did not matter to me where they went to high school. I just wanted to help them realize their dream.

I was not the type of coach who would send all his players to one university. Redan was a pipeline for sending quality athletes with integrity to college, but never all of them to one college program.

My approach to getting a kid into college was to match his skills and personality with the needs of a college program and the ability of the coach to give that kid that special something the player needed to develop into adulthood.

I believe the job of a coach at any level is to prepare young people for adulthood. Each of our young people will be turning into professionals; it just won't be in athletics.

I looked for coaches who could finish the job that I had begun in the young people who came through the Redan baseball program. Matching players with coaches is the hardest part of mentoring a kid in selecting which university experience will benefit his lifetime goals.

Not once would I dare try to decide for a student-athlete. I merely sought to provide options for deserving individuals.

You don't want to be responsible for selling a kid on a particular program, and the school doesn't work out. The decision of where one goes to college should be made by the student-athlete, with input, of course, from their parents or guardians. I think coaches should only serve as the conduit.

It is a source of much pleasure when a student graduated from the Redan baseball program and was heading off to complete the remainder of his education.

I continued assisting Marvin Pruitt, the coach who took over the Redan baseball program find college homes for our student-athletes. Pruitt became one of my best friends.

When I run into one of my students later in life, and they have miles of smiles on their faces, I cannot help but show off a big smile, too, from the exhilaration in knowing that a lot of hard work, years ago, went into producing those smiles.

I have had a lot of success coaching baseball at Redan High School.

Many accolades have come my way, including being named as the youngest and first African American to be selected for the Georgia Dugout Club Hall of Fame.

Perhaps, the most memorable thing in my coaching career and even in my playing days happened on the Redan baseball field one day in 1992 during the middle of my high school coaching career.

I was hitting fungo to the infielders. I noticed the outfielders were running around in the outfield. I yelled out to them to stop; the outfielders told me that a young kid was throwing rocks at them. I told them to go and catch him.

After a good chase, they caught the kid and brought him to me. The boy, David Jackson, lived with his mother down the street from the Redan baseball field.

He was about eight years old and had a learning disability. I asked him why he was throwing rocks at my players, and he told me that he did not have anything to do.

I asked him if he wanted to be my ball boy. He agreed to be the team ball boy, retrieve foul balls, and bring them back to the playing field. One of the best decisions that I have ever made was to make Dave an official Redan Raider.

Meeting young David Jackson taught me a big lesson I used when I became a high school administrator.

Whether they have a learning disability or no learning disability, young people will stay out of trouble if you give them a wholesome outlet to channel their energy positively.

Now, Dave was a part of the team and eventually my family. My kids loved him; the school kids loved him.

He soon enrolled into the Middle Grove Middle School's special education division and successfully graduated.

Next, he enrolled at Redan High School in the "special education" program. Dave received his high school diploma in 2001.

At Redan High School, Dave hung out with me every day. He became like a son to me. I took him on his first airplane ride.

Greg "Goody" Goodwin and Dave Jackson at the 2021 MVP Tournament. Photo ©2021 Cascade Publishing House

We flew to North Carolina in 2003 when Dave was 21 years old to play in a baseball tournament for kids with disabilities, aptly named "The Miracle League."

Chan Proctor started the Miracle Baseball League. It is a league for young people with disabilities.

Chan was one of my former players at Redan High School. Another story about relationships and how they continue to bless my life. Chan played baseball at The Citadel before becoming a successful businessman in Charleston.

## "G-O-O-D-Y"

Dave had a lot of fun playing baseball. I enjoyed watching him play as much as I have enjoyed any of the many baseball games I have coached or seen in my life.

It was a thrilling experience for Dave, and I was excited to share those moments with him for the remainder of his life.

I took Dave to many places to expose him to as much of life as possible.

My grandfather had a fantastic guy named James "Red" Williams that he supported much of his life, and when my grandfather died, my Uncle Jim took him in to care for him.

"Red" had a learning disability as well. I was around "Red" while growing up in Tulsa. "Red" was one of my favorite people.

I learned so much about life from "Red" and dealing with adversity as we worked side by side at the Eagle's office during my youth. "Red" was family.

When we host the MVP tournament during the summer, Dave would help to keep the Georgia State Baseball Complex in tip-top shape. He is known as the Chief Executive Officer of MVP. Regrettably, Dave passed in his sleep, June 20, 2022. We will miss his carefree disposition at the MVP Tournament.

## "G-O-O-D-Y"

Redan High School pays tribute to Dave Jackson.

Photo © 2022 Harold Michael Harvey

# Part Five
# Dream Maker

## "G-O-O-D-Y"

At the close of the 1999-2000 school year, my principal, Mr. Willie McGrady, came to me and asked if I wanted to leave the classroom and the dugout to become his assistant principal. He said he found that coaches made good administrators; after all, a coach manages the needs of a team, on and off the field. The school is just a bigger team.

As I went about my duties, the principal scouted me; measured my ability to meet the challenges on and off the field.

An adage says, always put your best foot forward because you never know when a scout is in the stands, observing how you perform the game's tasks. When I first came to Miller Grove Junior High School, I had hall duty. Coach Clark and I would sit in the front hallway and keep the students in line.

We bantered back and forth with each other in a cheerful kind of way, and when we had to discipline a youngster in the hallway, we did it joyfully and compassionately. All we wanted from the students was compliance with the rules of acceptable behavior. We were not out to embarrass, nor to humiliate a student in front of school peers.

I was reluctant to say yes to Mr. McGrady. When Coach Clark had asked me to become his assistant coach and later recommended me for the head coaching position when he left to coach on the collegiate level, I thought I had found my niche. I was of the mindset that I would teach and coach baseball until retirement.

Working with young girls and guys and teaching life skills during a baseball or softball game was enjoyable and fulfilling. Coaching provided a service to my community by encouraging young people to think about college after high school and finding scholarship money to fund their development into productive American citizens.

Giving back to one's community does not get any better than this; at least, that is how I thought at that time.

Life was good. Why complicate matters by adding extra responsibilities in school management?

Besides that, we were coming off the worst season regarding wins and losses in my coaching career. Our record in 2000 was 10-14-2. I was anxious and enthusiastic about rebuilding the program for the next season.

I knew we were capable of rebounding, and I was busy making plans to get back to our winning ways. The Junior Varsity had had a great year and had a "young stud" entering the ninth grade by the name of Chris Nelson.

The future looked bright to recapture our winning ways at Redan. Nelson would enjoy a stellar Redan High School career, capping it off by accepting an offer from the Colorado Rockies. He was the ninth pick in the first round of the 2004 Major League draft.

I continued to resist McGrady's offer to become the assistant principal. As a school administrator, Mr. McGrady told me that I could impact more students by encouraging the entire student body to aspire to be more and do more.

Since I had become an expert in getting scholarships for baseball players, I could help other kids reach their college education goals. The offer made a lot more sense to me after hearing his explanation.

What better gift can daughters give the baseball dad—
a photo from the Goodwin collection.

He almost had me, but the allure of baseball was firm in my blood. Then the principal said that while I was helping other kids obtain college scholarships, I would have to pay for my daughters' college education. He said it made more sense to pay for their education on a school administrator's salary than on the income of a high school teacher and baseball coach.

His counsel caused me to take stock of my family situation. I had been focused on helping to make other children successful.

It had not dawned on me in such a profound way I had two beautiful daughters who would need the same opportunities I was providing children in the Redan community.

    The principal also hinted that he would retire in a few years, and the school would need good leadership to answer the challenges of the twenty-first century.

    His argument made sense to me. Then I took stock of the fact that my wife received a promotion in 1998 to the position of Vice President at the Federal Reserve Bank.

    So maybe it was time for me to advance my career in education. I hesitantly agreed to leave the classroom and the dugout and accept the position of assistant principal.

From L-R: Greg "Goody" Goodwin, Brooke Ashleigh Goodwin, Cynthia Goodwin, and Lindsey Erin Goodwin. Photo from the Goodwin Collection.

Today my daughters are doing well. Brooke Ashleigh Goodwin followed us to Tennessee State University. She lives in Los Angeles and has a rewarding career as a major department store chain buyer.

Her sister Lindsay Erin Goodwin received her college degree from Florida A & M University. She has a career as a flight attendant with American Airlines. They have both been such exceptional children: minimal problems and have provided maximum love. I am so proud to be their father.

## "G-O-O-D-Y"

In large part, I owe most of their success to their mother, who was the ultimate coach's wife and an amazing mother. Most coaches at the high school and college level spend an excessive amount of time looking out for the children of other parents in their respective communities. I owed my daughters the same opportunities and I am so grateful to my wife and their mom for stepping in for me as I coached three sports for several years. I had a lot of ball games and late nights, but we made it work.

Before becoming an assistant principal, I assisted Principal McGrady in the search for a baseball coach who could continue Redan's quest for a state championship. We found that coach in Marvin Pruitt.

He was a veteran coach. And an amazing man, He led several baseball programs with excellence. Those programs were Lakeside, Rockdale, Southwest Dekalb, and Stephenson High School.

I agreed with Principal McGrady regarding who my successor would be. Coach Pruitt edged out a young coach by the name of Paris Burd who I have mentored and has become one of my closest friends.

In short, Burd currently serves as the Middle School Athletic Director for the Dekalb County School District and assists with the MVP tournament each year.

Coach Pruitt was more than up for the challenge. In 2013, Coach Pruitt rewarded the Redan Nation's confidence in him with the state championship trophy, a convincing sweep of Marist High School. When he closed out his coaching career the following year, he was the winningest baseball coach in Dekalb County history with a record of 447-252, a .640 winning percentage.

Coach Pruitt also became a member of the Georgia Dugout Club Hall of Fame. Our daily conversations with Coach Pruitt were priceless as he included me in discussions as he guided the Redan Baseball program.

I was saddened when the legendary Coach Marvin Pruitt departed this earth in 2019. I lost a great friend, and the world lost a great man.

As much as I looked forward to growing as a school administrator, I was elated to remain in baseball.

I developed a relationship with several professional baseball scouts during my tenure as the head coach at Redan. Fortunately, we had several young men drafted during my time as the Head Baseball Coach.

When Scout John Castleberry heard that I might be stepping down from my coaching duties, he immediately recommended that I become his part-time assistant for the Miami Marlins (Florida Marlins); it took me no time to accept the part-time scouting job.

I scouted for them from 2000 to 2002. Castleberry has worked for several clubs in his scouting career. He is currently with the San Francisco Giants.

With a change of scouting directors, many scouts are either let go or relocate to other clubs. I was fortunate to survive such an organizational change. The Marlins and I departed ways after 2002.

In 2003, one of my best friends, Clarence Johns, was elevated to a full-time scouting position with the Colorado Rockies. Johns had been a part-time guy with the Los Angeles Dodgers.

He recommended me to Lon Joyce for his old job. Joyce and I previously knew each other. So, I secured the position and scouted for the Dodgers from 2003 through 2017.

Scouting put me back into baseball, my sports passion. I traveled the southeast, placing an eye on the talent in the region.

We drafted and signed quite a few players during this time, and I was blessed to see many baseball games. I could write another book just with stories about my time as a part-time baseball scout. Who knows, maybe I will. I shared with Tim Osborne, a scouting buddy, some hilarious times. He worked several years with the Major League Baseball Scouting Bureau.

Greg "Goody" Goodwin with the radar gun scouting a young prospect. Photo from the Goodwin collection.

His tryout camps were something to behold. Young men who hadn't made their high school teams were trying out to become professional baseball players. It made for some exciting days, and thankfully no one got hurt.

At Redan, we were a large high school, so we had four assistant principals when the school board hired me. One of the assistant principals at Redan is called the disciplinary principal.

My primary duty would be as the disciplinary principal. The chief function of the punitive principal is to handle disciplinary issues at the school—my role included the morning duty, hall duty, and bus duty, as well as school discipline.

My role as the hall monitor when I became Coach Clark's assistant baseball coach came in handy.

I demonstrated the ability to discipline the students and remain a respected teacher and coach.

This may have been why I came to Mr. McGrady's attention as a potential school administrator.

As the disciplinary assistant principal, I brought everything I had been taught about discipline by my parents, high school, and college baseball teachers and coaches. I was also fortunate to have some outstanding prior principals at Redan, including Doyle Oran, Percy Mack, Willie McGrady, and Andrew Tatum.

During my tenure as the disciplinary assistant principal, I ensured the students knew that all we expected of them was to come to school, be on time, do what they were supposed to do, and mind "THEIR" business.

Greg "Goody" Goodwin was settling into the role of Redan High School Principal. Photo from the Goodwin collection.

## "G-O-O-D-Y"

If they did those "FOUR" things, I promised them they would not have any disciplinary problems, and success would be their reward.

The students who chose to follow my advice had an uneventful experience.

Those students who went astray had to deal with consequences.

In life, as in athletics, every action has its consequences. I learned this lesson growing up in Tulsa in my parents' home. My teachers and coaches reinforced this principle in school.

I knew that "tough" love works, and I incorporated tough love into my management style, as a high school baseball coach and administrator. Discipline is a good thing. You must have discipline, and I am a firm believer that discipline drives athletics and academics.

There is a tricky part about the duties of an assistant principal.

Sometimes a student's behavior can lead to an out-of-school suspension.

When it did, I had enough love for the student to exercise my power of discipline in hopes of impressing upon the student unsocial behavior was detrimental to the community and not tolerated in the Redan community or any civilized society. I would remind the student that I was not disciplining them. I had no choice but to punish their inappropriate behavior.

Even when disciplining a student, I did not want that student walking the street to get into trouble, leading to criminal intervention.

I developed a partnership with Vance Harper, the proprietor of Nick's Barber Shop on the corner of Redan and Hairston Roads in Stone Mountain, Georgia. The barbershop became a considerable part of the Redan experience during my tenure.

Harper was a former correctional officer who grew tired of seeing young Black men locked up inside prison walls, so he quit his job and opened a barbershop where he reached out to mentor the young males who came into the barbershop for a haircut.

I dropped in one day in 1993 after hearing several of my students talk about the barbershop. I have been a regular there ever since.

I noticed how Harper interacted with the youngsters in his shop. He was dropping words of wisdom but did not spare his tongue when chastising a kid for outlandish behavior.

I believed Harper could reach some of Redan's more troublesome students. I asked him if he would help mentor some of our kids when we suspended them from school.

Mr. Harper agreed to give the students a job in his barbershop during the length of the suspension.

Of course, this mentorship at Nick's was agreed upon by the students and parents.

Another prerequisite to participate in this mentoring program was all school work must be completed before reporting to the barbershop each day during their suspension.

Harper put the students to work sweeping the floor, washing the windows, and cleaning out the barber chairs, of which Nick's Barber Shop had fifteen.

When their suspension was over, the kids were encouraged to continue their part-time job in the barbershop.

Harper, and the other barbers, peppered the students with positive encouragement in between the student's work assignments.

Discussion topics included personal appearance and lessons in talking to other people, including respecting their parents and teachers.

A variety of people in Dekalb County came to Harper's shop for a haircut and discussed the significant issues of the day.

A chess club offered youngsters a way to resolve conflict by thinking several steps ahead of the current moment.

Harper helped us save and change hundreds of lives by giving young people a strong dose of tough love in his barbershop.

Some of those men and a few women are successful in law, and medicine. Other professions included: firefighters, preachers, teachers, carpenters, and plumbers.

Nick's Barber Shop was the unofficial Country Club for the Redan High community.

Back in the day so many influential people came through Nick's barber shop. A young aspiring lawyer named Hank Johnson was a regular customer and mentor to our kids. Johnson later become a congressman.

Community mentors who frequented Nick's Barber Shop and helped guide the teenagers were:

Rev. Attorney Bernice King, Judge Vincent Crawford, Comedian Chris Tucker, chess masters Beauregard Hardeman and Eddie Kemp, artist Jimmi Claybrook, rapper Archie, State Representative Billy Mitchell, entrepreneur David Waters, and newspaper publisher Dr. Earl Glenn.

These were the caliber of people who were regular patrons at Nick's Barber Shop.

They were wise to the world's ways, and adding to the political discourse, they proved to be excellent mentors for the young men and women I sent there from Redan to understand society's rules better.

Harper was a master of the "tough love" approach that I had experienced as a child growing up and at every stage of my development.

If we showed young people first that we love them, we could teach them a better way to navigate their way through life.

We could save many of them from the jailhouse—Harper and the men he employed as barbers were masters of tough love.

This experience was more evidence that it does "take a village to raise a child."

A few of Harper's barbers had their brush with the law in their younger years. They knew what awaited an undisciplined young Black man full of himself and angry at the world.

Sometimes they used harsh terms to shake up a kid. The language was rough but always sprinkled with love, insight, and a better way of getting along with other people who inhabit the same planet.

Words which we couldn't use in the schoolhouse but were heard often in the streets and some homes kept the conversation colorful and authentic.

Terms the kids understood and related to their experience.

I required the parents to deliver their students to the barbershop after completing schoolwork each day during their suspension. I would go by and check on them.

Nick's Barber Shop chess club. Photo from the Vance Harper Collection.

At other times, members of my staff would drop by to check on the students. Harper would give me a report on the progress of each student we sent to him.

Although I suspended students from school, I can walk in the Redan neighborhood without fear of any former student or parent being angry.

We made sure each student we disciplined knew that we loved them, even as we disciplined them for their inappropriate behavior. Eventually, the students understood why they had to be suspended.

In February 2006, Mr. Tatum retired. Tatum had assumed the role of Principal after Mr. McGrady retired in 2002. I had been his assistant for four years.

He recommended me to the regional superintendent as his replacement.

Because Mr. Tatum retired before the 2005-2006 academic school year ended, I was elevated as the interim principal while the Superintendent determined who they would name as the permanent principal.

Mr. McGrady had selected me for school administration, and Mr. Tatum had groomed me to be his replacement. However, it was not a forgone conclusion that I would be his replacement. As fate would have it, after the interview process, I was offered the position and accepted it.

Each principal brings a specific theme to their school. My motto was **"Ordinary people doing extraordinary things."**

## "G-O-O-D-Y"

In the beginning, I wanted to impress on the faculty and staff that each of us was an ordinary person who had an opportunity to do extraordinary things in the life of the students whom the state had charged us to serve.

Having been a veteran educator for twenty-one years, I knew that a principal was only as good as his staff. Principals only manage the school setting.

Schools are run by great assistant principals, aided by caring secretaries, diligent counselors, courageous teachers, hardworking coaches, marvelous cafeteria workers, and meticulous custodians that keep the building clean. All those positions I mentioned are severely underpaid.

Educators and education workers have been undervalued and under-appreciated in American society for years. Of course, I heard for years the nonsense that anyone can teach and how great it is that educators have summers off.

Most folks couldn't last a day in a classroom, and educators who are not working a job in the summer to make ends meet, need that rest to prepare for the next school year. It is a challenging but rewarding career.

Our country experienced the difficulty and challenges of teaching when forced to teach their children through virtual learning during the Covid-19 Pandemic of 2020. I genuinely believe that people now respect and appreciate the work of educators.

Next, I wanted to instill in the student body that they could achieve extraordinary things in life as ordinary people. Sure, some people are born with certain advantages, but eventually, everyone will have to walk in and create their paths.

It was important to me that my staff understood we were all part of a team. I knew that my leadership would be an extension of coaching.

I wanted to ensure the cafeteria and custodial staff realized that there were no extraordinary people in the building.

Everybody was just ordinary people striving to accomplish extraordinary things. I hoped to empower them to do incredible things to make the school community flourish. We were all part of the team. Of course there were policies, procedures, and a hierarchical tree that had to be followed.

I taught my students what my family had taught me: That all people were equal, that the janitor mattered as much as the librarian, the teachers, and the principal. More importantly, while the administrators and staff mattered, I wanted my students to know that they mattered equally.

Before my tenure, Redan High School had a long and distinguished history. I love Redan High. I owe the school community a lot. They embraced and supported my efforts. Redan allowed me to be the first Black baseball coach in school history.

When I took over the baseball team, I wanted to make an excellent baseball program into a superlative program.

Redan baseball rated high among the southeast's top high school programs in a few short years. After twelve seasons and a hall of fame coaching career, I was promoted to assistant principal where I served for six years. I then became principal in 2006.

My job was to continue the outstanding educational service Redan received accolades for providing. I wanted to expand the Redan footprint throughout the country on the collegiate and corporate level.

To accomplish my plans for Redan High School would require an outstanding faculty, custodial, and dietary staff. Please understand I am including our security personnel when I use the term faculty. It takes all three components to provide the best educational experience possible for a school to be successful. And we had an exceptional team at Redan.

The staff is the key to a school's success. The most trouble I got into as a principal was with the kitchen personnel. They were serious about providing wholesome meals to the students.

They made sure that every student ate lunch. If a student was not eating, the cafeteria ladies were at my door telling me something was wrong with a student, or a student didn't eat.

Unfortunately, some of these kids' only meals came from the nutrition they would receive at school.

Every person in the building was required to respect the custodial and dietary staff. Respect for everyone is a lesson I learned from my father.

He taught me that "you are only as good as the people around you, and the people around you are everybody."

Of course all students were not respectful, but they were disciplined for rude and disrespectful behavior.

We recognized that every student has their path, so we did not preach college to everybody, only to the students interested in college.

We did not push all our kids into athletics, but we worked hard to provide an excellent sports program for those who wanted it. If a kid wanted to be a mechanic, we encouraged them to apply themselves and make their dreams come true. Whatever a student wanted to do in life; we encouraged them to pursue it with a passion.

During my tenure as principal, Redan received recognition as a school of excellence. We could not have accomplished this feat if all three components did not provide an excellent learning environment.

In 2012 I received the Horace Tate Leadership Award from Emory University's Educational Studies Department.

I owe a debt of gratitude to Dr. Vanessa Siddle-Walker and Dr. Sheryl Croft for including me in as a Fellow in the Teaching in the Urban South (TITUS) Program.

In 2013, the Dekalb School District Region III selected me as the Principal of the Year for the 2012-2013 school year. I retired as the principal of Redan High School after the 2014-2015 school year.

None of this would have been possible without tremendous staffers. I would like to take this opportunity to thank and salute all the many individuals who made it possible for me to receive those accolades.

I had been the principal for nine of my 30 year career in education. At the time I was one of the longest-serving principals on the south side of Dekalb County.

During my time as principal, Redan had the fifth highest graduation rate in the district, and I led the school during its transition to Title I status.

This simply means the school community was transiting from upper middle class to working poor and would receive more government funds to support our students.

When I became principal at Redan High School I believed that my obligation was to help children. I think I did that; it didn't matter what color - I always wanted to make sure the children realized their potential.

Despite not being in the dugout anymore, I began to hear the narrative that Black kids were no longer playing baseball. From my experience as a high school baseball coach and scout, I knew this was not true.

However, I was disturbed about the dwindling number of Black players in Major League Baseball.

The Champion Newspaper ran a story on my retirement in 2015.

I could have ignored this situation. But I was good friends with several like-minded individuals who all felt that we could create a tournament that featured minority and other underserved high school young men annually.

We sought to increase the opportunities for these young men to gain exposure to professional scouts and college recruiters.

I met with several baseball enthusiasts: including Paris Burd, Greg Davis, Milton Sanders, Melvin Traynum, Clarence Johns, Danny Montgomery, and Steve Williams.

We formed MVP, the Mentoring Viable Prospects organization to play a baseball tournament for emerging predominately Black high school players in the metro Atlanta area in 2005.

Johns, Montgomery, and Williams worked full-time in the major league baseball industry.

They connected us to the legendary Chicago Simeon High School coach, Leroy Franklin, Kenny Fullman, and Rob Fletcher from Chicago, Edward "Chip" Lawrence, another Major League executive from Florida, Manny Upton from Virginia, Darold Brown based out of California, and others who grew the game in African American communities throughout the country.

My scouting supervisor with the Los Angeles Dodgers, Lon Joyce, introduced me to former big leaguer Morris Madden; he was a significant player in the North Carolina youth baseball market. He brought a team from North Carolina to our annual tournament, and we became fast friends.

# "G-O-O-D-Y"

Hopefully, we have been difference makers. Since our inception as a 501 (c) 3 non-profit organization in 2005, MVP has assisted hundreds of young men in obtaining baseball scholarships to colleges throughout the country with a heavy emphasis on our Historically Black Colleges and Universities.

From our efforts, so many other organizations have formed, including The Chicago Ace program - in my opinion - is one of the best amateur programs in baseball for our kids.

Also in this category are the Major League Baseball's Break Through Series, Carolina Reds program in Charlotte, North Carolina, run by my good friend and former big league player Morris Madden.

Additionally, numerous other programs were started from MVP's humble efforts to increase participation in the African American communities, which include the Minority Baseball Prospect organization founded by Alex Wyche.

Milwaukee Brewers Special Assistant for Scouting "Chip" Lawrence brings a team to our tournament each year.

Lawrence founded the Pro-Youth Foundation, an organization based in Florida that has assisted hundreds of our youth in obtaining baseball scholarships and other opportunities in baseball. "Chip's" father, Edward Lawrence, Sr. signed a professional baseball contract with the Milwaukee Braves in 1957, the year I was born.

According to Coach Mark Salter, a protégé of John Young, a former Chicago Cubs scout and the person who developed the concept of Reviving Baseball In the Inner City (RBI) to Major League Baseball, the above-referenced programs followed what we were doing with the MVP.

Today, MVP is the oldest minority baseball tournament in the country. Each year we bring teams into Atlanta, Georgia from North Carolina, Virginia, Florida, Illinois, Texas, and California to compete in a three-day tournament. We invite area major league baseball scouts and baseball coaches from Historically Black Colleges and Universities to come out and assess the talent on the field.

Annually, we have head baseball coaches from many HBCUs. Schools in regular attendance include the following: Alabama State University, Alabama A & M University, Tuskegee University, Claflin College, North Carolina A & T University, Grambling State University, Alcorn State University, Prairie View State University, Southern University, and Jackson State University and Rust College among others attend our event. The coaches come with their stopwatches and radar guns to grade the elite talent in the Black baseball community.

Each year, several young men receive baseball scholarship offers from some of the county's top Black college baseball programs.

Additionally, scouts from many Major League franchisees review the talented Black kids playing baseball each year. The Atlanta Braves, Texas Rangers, and Colorado Rockies are some of the mainstays.

Each of them has signed professional prospects from participants in the MVP tournament.

In 2019, Brandon Baker worked with the ground crew readying the field for each game as part of his work-study job. He completed his graduate school studies at Georgia State University. Brandon was a member of the Redan High School 2013 State Championship team member,

Following his senior year of high school ball, Baker signed a scholarship offer with the University of Missouri. After he arrived, the head baseball coach found himself out of a job. The new coach did not keep any of the pitchers from the former coach. So, Baker was in a dilemma.

He had several offers coming out of high school, and he would transfer into the baseball program at Georgia State. He graduated with a bachelor's and master's degrees but no contract from a Major League franchise five years later.

Three days after receiving his Master's, Baker reported to his work study job as a groundskeeper for the Georgia State baseball program. His responsibility was to prepare the field for the MVP tournament, which he had played in during high school.

During the tournament, Baker came to me and asked me if it was possible to set up a tryout for him with a few of the professional scouts in attendance. I pointed out Clarence Johns, at that time, the Cross Checker for the Texas Rangers.

Johns was a founding member of MVP and a member of its board of advisors. I told him I would consult with Johns about the possibility of a tryout. I shared with Johns that Baker was a left-handed pitcher who had just exhausted his eligibility at Georgia State and that he was looking for an opportunity to continue playing baseball. Johns remembered Baker and agreed that the lefty deserved a chance to audition for a professional job.

In between games, Johns assembled five other scouts who were in attendance and told them he would work out a left-handed pitcher, and they were welcome to attend.

Baker went down to the bullpen and consistently threw 92 mph on the radar gun. He also displayed an excellent feel for his off-speed pitches. Fortunately for Johns, the other scouts had to contact their front office to offer Baker a contract.

Johns, as a cross-checker, had the authority to sign Baker on the spot. He did, and Baker's dream to become a professional baseball player came true.

Helping people realize their dreams is what I like about what I do. The agonizing part of coaching was seeing the end of young people's careers after their senior year ended.

Brandon Baker is signing a free-agent contract with the Texas Rangers. Photo from the Goodwin collection.

After my second year as a head coach and realizing I didn't have to endure this feeling, I began meeting with my seniors during the middle of the season to understand where they would head after high school.

Of course, the ones moving on to play in college were secure. I was relieved that several of my players had great parental support and were already accepted into colleges of their choice. Others had opted to join the military or the workforce.

A few had no clue, and those were the ones that needed my help and support. Through Redan's excellent support system: including Pam Cool, the school's front office secretary – but who wore many hats – and all my great assistant coaches along with amazing counseling staff, we got these young people headed in the right direction after high school.

I always felt blessed to be placed at Redan High. The staff was so accommodating, and it was indeed a family atmosphere.

Charlotte Joy, Yolanda Peek, Constance Franklin, Linda Cooley, Darlene Godbey, Janice Boger, Thelishia Wright, Lorenzo Moore, and many more teachers and staff helped push our school to unbelievable heights.

I would cap off my career in education when I was selected to serve as the interim athletic director for the Dekalb County School District, which served more than 100,000 young men and women in 2017.

The success of MVP is due to a large cadre of volunteers who come out each year to help put on this event.

Several of my baseball teammates from Tennessee State University, former college and professional baseball players, and coaches volunteer each year to help run the concession stand or to serve as ticket agents and generally make sure the tournament goes off without a hitch.

Here again, "you are only as good as the people around you, and the people around you are everybody." It takes the entire community of dedicated people to pull off the MVP tournament each year and give Black high school baseball players and underserved individuals a showcase to earn an opportunity to play the game we all love on the next level.

One of the many things I admired about Dave Jackson is that despite his learning disability, he put in a great deal of work during the MVP tournament to ensure that these kids have an opportunity that he could not enjoy.

This selfless dedication to other people makes Dave the MVP of this tournament. The kids and coaches who participate in the contest love Dave and ask about him years after participating.

During the pandemic year 2020, we decided to cancel the MVP tournament. The long-term health of the kids was of paramount importance to us.

After all, it is not about which team wins the tournament. From the start, it has given the kids a competitive spotlight to showcase their talent. We were blessed to resume the tournament in 2021.

I have a poster in our basement that sums up my approach to life, baseball, and school administration. The poster reads:

*"In this house, we root for each other, swing for the fences, never quit, try our hardest, keep our eye on the ball, throw three strikes, and you're out, believe in teamwork. In this house, we play baseball."*

I was born to serve and have enjoyed the service I have rendered to others. Catch the spirit, pay some rent for the space you occupy upon this earth. It does not cost anything to volunteer.

As stated earlier, "I hit the lottery at birth, being born to two amazing, loving families." I extended that fortune by selecting a college in Tennessee State University that encouraged us through the motto: "Think, work, and serve."

I was able to find a passion for helping young people and thriving in both education and athletics.

I currently enjoy semi-retirement in the metro Atlanta area, managing the Mentoring Viable Prospects (MVP) baseball organization. Also, serving as an advisor with the Marquis Grissom Baseball Association. Additionally, I enjoy my volunteer service with the Georgia Dugout Club.

Martin Luther King, Jr. said it best and summed up what I shared about my life with his quote.

*"Everybody can be great... because anybody can serve. You don't have to have a college degree to serve. You don't have to make your subject and verb agree to serve. You only need a heart full of grace. A soul generated by love."*

The Greg Goodwin family pictured from L-R is Lindsey Erin Goodwin, Brooke Ashleigh Goodwin, Cynthia Goodwin, and "Goody." Photo from the Goodwin collection.

I was able to meet and marry my beautiful, intelligent, and talented wife, Cynthia.

## "G-O-O-D-Y"

Together we raised two extraordinary, caring young ladies in Brooke and Lindsay. This journey has been a fantastic ride. I hope yours has been as well. We all have a story, and this is mine.

# Postscript

**G****reg Goodwin** is the "godfather" of black baseball in the city and a true team player supporting every up-and-coming coach and program I know exists!

He runs MVP and has allowed many high school prospects to advance to collegiate and professional careers.

Danielle Bedasse

Director, Community Affairs and Executive Director, Atlanta Braves Foundation

**Greg Goodwin** has that infectious personality that truly meets no stranger. His spirit is all about helping others more than trying to receive accolades or praise for his works. His favorite line he uses is: "It's about the kids," and honestly, that quote is Greg to a tee.

There is never a doubt when he is around because he is truly loud, and his voice carries. He makes my day when we connect with immense fun and laughter, love, Greg, eternal.

### Dan Montgomery
Assistant General Manager/Vice President of Scouting, Colorado Rockies

**Greg Goodwin** is a selfless, dedicated stalwart whose unwavering commitment to future generations has been unparalleled.

Clarence Johns II 20-year MLB scouting veteran Currently VP of Baseball Operations Munger English Sports Management

# Photographs

Greg "Goody" Goodwin mentoring kids at Chip Lawrence's Pro Youth Foundation Showcase in Kansas City, Missouri, July 23, 2021. Photo from the Goodwin Collection.

"G-O-O-D-Y"

President Joe Biden and Oklahoma State Rep. Regina Goodwin. Photo The Goodwin collection.

Regina Goodwin, Greg Goodwin, and Sabrina Goodwin Monday Photo from the Goodwin collection.

Greg "Goody" Goodwin and Roland Martin during 2021 centennial observance of the Tulsa Race Massacre. Photo The Goodwin Collection.

Greg Goodwin and Regina Goodwin at the door of no return during a visit to Goree Island, Ghana. Photo from the Goodwin collection.

During a 2018 visit to Goree Island, my thoughts immediately made me think of the sacrifices our people made. It was one of the most emotional moments of my life. Photo from the Goodwin collection.

Edward "Goody" Goodwin and Greg "Goody" Goodwin are sharing a laugh, a passion of both men. Photo from the Goodwin collection.

From L-R: Regina Goodwin, Alquita Parker Goodwin, And Sabrina Goodwin Monday. Photo from the Goodwin Collection

Greg "Goody" and Mama Alquita Parker Goodwin. Photo from the Goodwin collection.

## "G-O-O-D-Y"

Sabrina Goodwin Monday, Regina Goodwin, and Greg "Goody" Goodwin. Photo from the Goodwin Collection.

Regina Goodwin, Alquita Goodwin, and Sabrina Goodwin Monday. Photo from the Goodwin collection.

Regina Goodwin, Sabrina Goodwin Monday, and Greg Goodwin Photo from the Goodwin collection.

My last baseball game with my dad and lifelong friend Kenneth Wayne Jones in St. Louis during the 2013 season. Daddy passed later that year. Kenneth passed in 2019. Enjoy family and friends. We are all only passing through. Photo from the Goodwin collection.

## "G-O-O-D-Y"

Georgia Congressman Hank Johnson, Oklahoma State Representative Regina Goodwin and Greg Goodwin. Photo from the Goodwin collection.

Sabrina Goodwin Monday, Congressman Hank Johnson, St. Rep. Regina Goodwin, and Greg "Goody" Goodwin. The photo is from the Goodwin collection.

Regina Goodwin makes a point during a family discussion with Greg Goodwin in the conference room, which doubles as the kitchen at the old homestead in Tulsa. Photo from the Goodwin collection

Greg Goodwin clowning with Bernard Pattillo, former City of Atlanta Director of Recreation during the 2021 MVP Tournament.

©2021 Cascade Publishing House

# "G-O-O-D-Y"

Legendary NBA basketballer Craig Hodges and Greg "Goody" Goodwin are taking a break during the filming of a documentary on Hodges. Photo from the Goodwin Collection

Greg "Goody" Goodwin with baseball royalty Henry Aaron and two Redan baseball coaches, Chris Hardnett and Delwyn Patterson. Photo from the Vance Harper collection

From L-R Steve Williams, Director of Professional Scouting Pittsburgh Pirates, Danny Montgomery, Assistant General Manager Colorado Rockies, Tyrone Brooks, Vice President Major League Baseball and Greg Goodwin (just a guy).

Former Major League General Manager Bill Bavasi shares thoughts on the game of baseball to kids attending 2021 WWBA National Championship. The Atlanta team lost one game in the tournament to the eventual tournament winner.

## "G-O-O-D-Y"

Greg "Goody" Goodwin is in a contemplative mood.
Photo from the Goodwin collection.

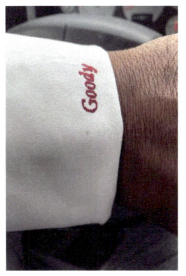

The cuffs say it all—a photo from the Goodwin
collection.

Coach Goody Goodwin sharing a bit of baseball knowledge and life skills during a baseball camp at Redan High School. Matt Olsen, 2021 MLB All-Star is pictured standing with other professional players behind Goodwin. November 7, 2021. Photo from the Goodwin collection.

From L-R Tony Reagins, VP MLB, Dale Matthews, Coordinator of Youth Sports MLB, Danny Montgomery, Assistant General Manager, Colorado Rockies, and just a guy from Cherryvale Kansas, Greg "Goody" Goodwin. Photo from the Goodwin collection.

"G-O-O-D-Y"

The Baseball field at Redan High School is now the Greg Goodwin Field. Photo from the Goodwin Collection.

# About the Author

**Greg "Goody" Goodwin** grew up in Tulsa, Oklahoma. He is a descendant of the 1921 Tulsa Race Massacre survivors, a third-generation graduate of the Booker T. Washington High School in Tulsa.

He earned a Bachelor of Science Degree in Government and Public Affairs and a Master's in Public Administration from Tennessee State University. "Goody" is an avid baseball influencer, a former baseball player, teacher, coach, professional baseball scout, and high school principal.

"Goody" has rendered service to several thousand young people during his professional life. His motto "play to win" typifies the passion he brings to serving humanity.

# About The Editor

**H**arold Michael Harvey is the *Living Now* 2020 Bronze Medal winner for his memoir *Freaknik Lawyer: A Memoir on the Craft of Resistance.* He is the author of a book on Negro Leagues Baseball, *The Duke of 18th & Vine: Bob Kendrick Pitches Negro Leagues Baseball.* He writes feature stories for *Black College Nines. Com.* Harvey is a member of the Collegiate Baseball Writers Association, HBCU and PRO Sports Media Association, and the Legends Committee for the National College Baseball Hall of Fame. Harvey is an engaging speaker. Contact Harvey at hmharvey@haroldmichaelharvey.com.